AF830915

OH BLOGGER!

TRAVELLERS

MP's & COUNCILLORS

OH BLOGGER!

FastPrint Publishing
www.fast-print.net/store.php

Oh Blogger!
Copyright © Wayne Shaw 2013

ISBN: 978-178035-616-7

All rights reserved

No part of this book may be reproduced in any form by photocopying or any electronic or mechanical means, including information storage or retrieval systems, without permission in writing from both the copyright owner and the publisher of the book.

The right of Wayne Shaw to be identified as the author of this work has been asserted by him in accordance with the Copyright, Designs and Patents Act 1988 and any subsequent amendments thereto.

A catalogue record for this book is available from the British Library

First published 2013 by
FASTPRINT PUBLISHING
Peterborough, England.

An environmentally friendly book printed and bound in England by www.printondemand-worldwide.com

Mixed Sources
Product group from well-managed forests, and other controlled sources
FSC www.fsc.org Cert no. TT-COC-002641
© 1996 Forest Stewardship Council

PEFC Certified
This product is from sustainably managed forests and controlled sources
PEFC PEFC/16-33-415
www.pefc.org

This book is made entirely of chain-of-custody materials

OH BLOGGER!

ACKNOWLEDGEMENTS & THANK YOU

Data protection / Street ear cleaners / Bird droppings / Knut Fest / Mr. Donkey / British Pubs / Mayan Calendar / The Honey Monster / Gary McKinnon / Geocaching / All the "Stans" / Jabber Jabber Jabber / Bank Holidays / MP's Pay Review / Pigeon English / Immigration / Housing / Cane Rats / National Pirate's day / Magistrates Courts / Mrs DJ Wayne for feeling the love / Politicians all over the world without whom this book would not be possible / Councils and councillors across the UK / The EU for giving us all a right good laugh / Nyces / Carl / David Bailey / Marmite and the Pussyratz / Marcel P and the Deltaphonics / Laffinboy Music / Ade Pierce / Anal sex and fetish perversion company / BBC World News / Disposable Penis / Peterborough Telegraph / Fast Print Publishing / The Englishman / Nudists / Travellers / Immigration control / The Euro / Street artists / Court Interpreters / Magistrates Courts / Ministry of Transport / Fly Tippers / Mathew Onyskiw / Retail opening hours / Message in a bottle / Plebgate / Human rights / Big issue vendors / National Health Service / Steven Brocklehurst / Totnes / Fanny eaters / Overseas aid / Insurance companies / Team GB / Jose Mujica / Free speech / Blackboard penis / Andrew Lyall Pointon / Gangham style / TV licence / Toby Flood / Spongebob Squarepants / £10,000 / Proof of age / Private Eye / Ukrainian / West Coat Franchise / Rocket Jump / Amplified / Alice / Jeanie / Milking / Stepan Piryanyk / Town Planners / Polish / Killiecrankie / Pinkie / Philiphaugh / Prestonpans / Sheriffmur / Blue / Garry the goat / Tesco / Grandmothers / Hajib / The Gambia / Drive through restaurants / Sydney Australia / Kangaroos / Colette / You Tube / Frogbeat / Female Clippy / Vanburger / Wombats / Mexican takeaways / Cheryl at Silverstone / Fat Cats / Benbecula / Scumbag Hackers / Tailgaters / Video Cassettes / Dr. Beeching / Whale Vomit / Iraq / London congestion charge / SSR Bash / Team GB / Iceberg lettuce / Bankstown Sydney Australia / Collingwood Melbourne Australia / Elizabeth S.A. / Airports / Baggage security / Pedestrian crossings / Newcastle NSW / Vehicle dealerships / Grease monkeys / facebook / Procrastination / Nail Fungus / Spam / 7726 / Richard third / Smokies / Sorry / PPI Helpline / Naked Rambler / NHS / UK Border Agency / Cartoon Penis / Fiscal Cliff / Titus Corlatean / Bashar-Al-Assad / Horsemeat / Helena Torry / Palestinian bombers smuggled sperm / Pontiff / Snowball fights / I am a stupid bad tempered git who punches boys / School pupil harassment / Computer Porn / Use your loaf / No balls – No Gumption / Supermarket Manager / Oh Boris / UKIP / Disabled parking bays / Abu Qatada / Mali / Electric garage doors / Arab spring / Art

~~~~~

Other books by the author available from Amazon UK, Fast Print Publishing or
www.whittleseasurf.com

ISBN: 978-178035-367-8 Not so perfect cooking

ISBN: 978-178035-368-5 Chooooon Part 1 A pictorial journey with Seaford Surf Radio SSR

Coming soon – Chooooon Part 2 Spot the Vanburger

Twitter Blog Facebook YouTube

wayne@whittleseasurf.com Tel: 07850 216131
~~~~~

INTRODUCTION

Welcome avid reader to my latest book "Oh Blogger!" and I sincerely hope you enjoy the experience as you blog along day by day, week by week and month by month reading and exploring topics which may be closer to your heart than you initially thought.

The selections of rants and stories have all appeared in D J Wayne's daily blog which has a link from the home pages of Seafordsurf Radio SSR and Whittleseasurf. They express my thoughts on a number of subjects which have hit the headlines in 2012 / 2013 as well as a number of unbelievable events which I have come across and had to deal with.

You name it, call centres, insurance companies, bad drivers and stroppy retail assistants I have had it all! I hope it will generate discussion and provoke thought on subjects which are varied and interesting. Just like my first book "Not so perfect cooking" there is a mix of ingredients to captivate the imagination, flavours to spice it up and finally topped with a hint of sarcasm and wit.

And as if that was not enough there is a pinch of irony and downright honesty and truth, something which councillors and members of parliament may clearly be lacking. There is also the issue of immigration especially the possible mass influx of Bulgarian and Romanians flooding into the country creating a strain on our schools and an unwelcome burden on the welfare system.

The rants are heartfelt and to the point, with a clear look at the absurd goings on in Council chambers, law courts, estate agents, house building programs and of course the old turkey "elf and safety".

Also included are selected photographs which are favourites of mine or taken to enhance a point made in the blog. The blog commenced in July 2012 during the build-up to the main event of the year, no not the Olympics (although they were excellent) no, I mean the SSR bash held at the rugby club in Seaford on Saturday 28th July 2012.

At the bash the long awaited second publication "Chooooon the history of internet radio station SSR Part 1" was officially launched and what a rocky road that was to get it published by the due date. You will be able to pick up on some of the frustrations as you follow the blog day by day.

The book signing at the SSR summer bash went extremely well and you can still obtain your personal copy from Fast Print publishers http://www.fast-print.net/bookshop/1103/chooooon-part-one or via myself and I will arrange for your copy to be personally signed by the SSR DJs.

The personal writings in the blog are spontaneous and to the point. The subject matter is drawn from various places including television and radio news stations, newspaper editorials and what I have seen and heard on my travels throughout Towns, Cities and our beautiful countryside, that is, before the scumbag fly tippers and so called travellers get there!

The behaviour of some of our elected MP's and councillors does not go unnoticed either. You may be surprised and possibly astounded at what occurs around and the behaviour of some individuals goes unnoticed unless brought to your attention. We commence our journey on Monday 2nd July 2012 and cover the period up to Sunday 31st March 2013.

MONDAY 2ND JULY 2012

A big "thank you" to Producer Colette from Seafordsurf Radio for organising DJ Wayne's blog. You can catch me every Monday night, 8-10 pm, presenting the Whittlesea scene and heard segment which features some great tracks as well as the old favourites "On this day in history", and "The Letter B pub quiz". You can also see me on "You tube" presenting my alternative cook book "Not so perfect cooking" which is available for purchase from Fast Print Publishing, Seafordsurf books (Amazon) or just follow the link from the home page of Seafordsurf Radio and Whittleseasurf. A great read indeed!

My second book "Chooooon Part 1 A pictorial journey with Seaford Surf Radio " has been reviewed, yet again, by the publishers and there were some possible maybe perhaps copyright issues which are holding up publishing.

I have to ask the question how do publications like the national press get away with modifications to images when we are not allowed??? I remember a number of occasions where celebrity heads have been superimposed on other bodies. One rule for you and one rule for me! (Unless you have the money to counterclaim being sued) Anyway with the assistance of Producer Frogbeat we have made some changes and the draft PDF is back with the publishers. Watch this space for progress.

DJ Wayne relaxing with a well-deserved pint outside the SSR studio in the Fens!

Update 1: Chooooon Part 1 A pictorial journey with seafordsurf radio was published in July 2012.
Update 2: Coincidently in August 2012 Prince Harry was unfortunately pictured naked in a Hotel room in Las Vegas. Now I am sure the young Prince was having a ball and if it was you or me in that position nobody would bat an eyelid. The point is, only one newspaper "The Sun" published selected pictures whilst one, perhaps even more, printed "mock ups" of Harry's head on a naked body. Will they get sued for copyright? I think not. So it must be a case of "getting the small guy" and not playing on an even playing field. Pfftt!

TUESDAY 3RD JULY 2012

This true story is indicative of how today's customers view retail. Customers can be arrogant and abusive to the retail assistant for no apparent reason apart from the personal joy of upsetting someone. A customer went up to the counter in a well known retail store with an expensive hair treatment which she had picked up from one of the isles.

"Excuse me, this appears to be used. Do you have any others?" The retail assistant said, "I'm sorry, ma'am. We just finished putting our stock away. If that was the last one on the shelf, then it's the last one we have."

Customer: "Well, I suppose I'll get it anyway. I've never tried it before, but I pumped some out and it does feel very nice." To which the retail assistant answered, "Ma'am, were you the one that opened and used it?"

The customer replied, "Yes, but I had to see what it was like before I spent all this money on it! Now, are you sure there aren't any more in the back? I really don't want to buy something that's been used!" To my way of thinking the idiot customer should have been made to pay for the product but this is the society we live in.

WEDNESDAY 4TH JULY 2012

On the Monday night show there is a segment called "Rant with DJ Wayne", and this could be on any subject at all. It all depends on you the listeners, the watchers, the blogger and fellow ranters.

A recurring rant these days is vehicles on the road without side lights in poor or bad visibility. It does not have to be day break or dusk which causes listeners to rant about vehicles creeping up from behind or coming towards them.

It has rained more or less continuous now for over three months and when it rains visibility is so bad that lights need to be on to ensure the vehicle can be seen. But oh no not for some of the "numpties" on our roads who carry on driving as if they were in bright sunshine.

These "numpties" are inconsiderate and a downright nuisance on the roads. These are probably the same idiots who tail gate you as you stick to the speed limit which obviously they don't wish to do. Allegedly they are usually locals and, as soon as they get the opportunity they overtake, knowing full well there is not a fixed speed camera just around the corner. Where are the Police when you want them? These idiots, if caught, and that is a big IF, should be fined, banned from driving have their vehicles impounded and crushed. They will find it very difficult to tailgate or overtake sitting on a cube of tangled metal and vehicle parts!

A little harsh I may hear you say but these individuals are a nuisance and damn intimidating to all of us, why should we put up with it?

THURSDAY 5TH JULY 2012

Hot news! The euro zone is facing difficulty and they may need a bailout. Now let me see, they will be needing a few billion quid and the UK, who are NOT in the faltering euro zone, are willing to provide more than £10 billion to help out.

I am sure we will all have voted a big YES on that one. Oh that reminds me we are all contributing to the government austerity measures with reduction in Council services, reducing the Armed Forces and oh yes suffering VAT at an extortionate rate of 20%.

Now forgive me why are we giving money away and suffering ourselves. I will not even mention petrol prices! YET! But have you noticed the prices at the pump are creeping up yet again. As of today the cost of a litre (for those like me who are a little long in the tooth that is a pint and three quarters) is £1.38p WHAT?

I had an e-petition in place, which has some months still to run requesting the government changes its mind in propping up the failing Euro zone. Please sign and let's get this debated in the Commons. It seems to be every day there is another story of a bale out for yet another country in the "zone" Spain, Portugal, Greece, Ireland, Italy. Does this not prove beyond reasonable doubt that the Euro zone one currency does not work, and will never work? It is an excuse for these nations not to balance their books and be given, yes given a cash input to keep them going for a few more years although recently a few more months!

Each country should drop the euro and go back to their respective currency. Let them sort out their own issues and regulate their own prices and taxes. They will soon find out that there is not a bottomless pit of money which can be thrown at them when they whinge and wine they cannot make ends meet. Then get your own house in order and stop asking for other people's money, no let me rephrase that, stop asking for my money. The amount I pay in taxes and VAT should and must be distributed within the UK.

The news of the latest cuts in the Armed Forces is out today and what another shambles by the Government "advisers". I believe some may be communist infiltrators (ends in traitor!" and one day in years to come, you mark my words, details of a plot to destroy the Country will be revealed. The present salami cutting and amalgamations are ludicrous and these are the UK's finest. What the hell is going on?

The politicians' debate and waffle, the civil servants come up with ludicrous policies they have worked out on a back of a fag packet and the politicians grunt and groan some more.

Update 1: Wednesday 12th September 2012. German court backs euro zone's ESM "European Stability Mechanism" bailout fund, and the European fiscal treaty. Now, apart from having a stupid name it clears the way for unlimited funding of debt ridden euro zone states. Some 37,000 people had signed a petition to the court asking it to block the ESM and make it subject to a referendum, but this was totally ignored. The amount authorised is 500bn euro (£400bn) (BBC News Europe)
Update 2: Unfortunately my e-petition did not get the necessary votes to get it debated in the House of Commons, but that is not the end of the story.

FRIDAY 6TH JULY 2012

As the weekend approaches there is news that the government has not reached its target for building new houses. Besides the fact that the Country has so many unemployed and the building trade is in recession it is not really surprising and should not shock anyone apart from the government that is.

However, I have to ask the question. Do we really need more houses? Do we really need to build concrete jungles? Do we really need to build on flood plains and then wonder why we get flooded when the rivers burst their banks?

The answer to all these questions is a resounding and unequivocal NO! We do not need any more houses built on a grand scale in this Country. There are enough houses for everybody who needs them and wants them. Now I can hear you saying "What are you on about? There are thousands on the housing waiting list".

The answer is simple: Put a stop to wholesale immigration where anybody who lands in this Country is entitled to housing and benefits. If you look up and down any high street you will see businesses in accommodation which should be for residential purposes.

In every village, town and city there are properties which have been empty for years and the owners cannot be traced, compulsory purchase these and re-let for families who need them. The only stopping point is the government and local councillors have not got the guts and balls to do anything about it.

Yap yap yap splutter cough whinge and whine that is the governments and local authorities' policies!

Here are my recommendations:

1. Compulsory purchase all residential properties which have remained unoccupied for 5 years

2. Build on brown sites, reduce the red tape and provide assistance with any decontamination which may be required.

3. Rescind the law that we have to provide accommodation to immigrants.

4. Only allow immigration to those who have a job opportunity and somewhere to live, before they leave their country of origin

5. Businesses who use residential properties for their businesses should be given assistance to move to purpose built premises, which are in abundance.

6. Do not build any more wholesale business industrial sites, which remain empty for decades, until all existing ones are filled.

7. Reduce the numbers of Council houses which are empty and boarded up. This number is disgustingly high. Either re-furbish them or raise to the ground and sell to building contractors to rebuild.

8. Do NOT build on designated flood plains – they are there for a very good reason!

9. Do NOT build on green belt land

10. Just use your gumption and DO IT!

SATURDAY 7TH JULY 2012

OK the tennis is now heading towards its climax and tomorrow is the men's final, the showboat of the lawn tennis calendar. Murray V Federer! Scots v Swiss! Or is it British versus the rest of the world?

Now I am British and proud of it, I am also English and very proud of it. Strange how some Councils object to the English flag being displayed as "Nationalistic". You may well have to see the political make up of these Councils!!!

Anyway, the point is, I remember during a football world cup Murray stated that being Scottish he would support any team as long as it is not England, and here is me thinking England Scotland Wales and Northern Ireland are Team GB. How naive I must be. I support the right side I support Team GB, however support the loner Murray I think not.

Shame really as during my time with the British Army, (that is BRITISH Army) I befriended a young Scotsman who was seconded to the Royal Signals from The Scots Greys and proud of it.

The Scots Greys fought at Waterloo and had many battle honours. This is another regiment the government has previously disembowelled in the guise of cost cutting.

So Switzerland is neutral and so am I!

Update: On Tuesday 11th September 2012 Andy Murray became the first British tennis player for 64 years to win a grand slam in the USA. I am one of the first to be proud of this accomplishment and say "Well done Andy", it is great achievement for Britain and it is a great achievement for Scotland.

SUNDAY 8TH JULY 2012

Well the Swiss outplayed the Scot and hey what a hell of a match. One day perhaps one day!

A great weekend dodging the showers! Silverstone took a beating and our friend Cheryl will not be able to get out of the camp site car park until Monday morning at the earliest.

Saturday night on SSR was the legend that is Vanburger and what a treat that was again. Vanburger entertained us by telling true stories, with artistic licence, of his life thus far and the celebrities he has met along the way.

I thought the story about when he was with the post office was hilarious. This was the occasion he was on his way home, still wearing his uniform and displaying his badge, managed to get a free ride on a bus, which used to happen years ago. Not nowadays! The female "clippy" was busy so asked Van to take the ticket collections downstairs, and of course the likeable Van agreed. So after an hour, and with a pocket full of change he reached his stop to disembark, Need I go on??

Listen to the legend that is Vanburger with incredible stories of his life every Saturday night. I did offer to be his official auto biographer but hey I was too late that position has been taken.

Update 1: One day, perhaps one day! That one day was Tuesday 11th September 2012!

MONDAY 9TH JULY 2012

Hot news Cheryl is still at Silverstone bogged down in the camp site. She did wish to leave on Sunday afternoon after the race had finished but they just could not get the cars off the parking area, sorry bog! Luckily she had not taken the tent down so another nights camping was on the cards.

However the car is bogged down and there is only one tractor towing the cars off the field. What!!! We are hoping to see Cheryl back at work Tuesday, maybe.

Well the tennis has finished and Andy Murray was magnificent in defeat. Mrs DJ Wayne asked the question have I ever been to Scotland to see the wild Countryside and scenery and I answered no, but I have and I will briefly tell you all about it.

It was in my Army days when I served in the Royal Signals. We were relocated for six months on the Scottish island of Benbecula which is located between North and South Uist in the Outer Hebrides. We were providing communications for the Artillery. The only means of getting to the island was via a ferry or helicopter. As the ferry did not run every day the mail usually came in via helicopter.

Now our camp, which consisted of a number of spider huts, was very near the sea edge, and yes you are probably ahead of me, on some occasions the mail pouch got a little wet as it was ejected from the helicopter made its way inland just to be taken in the opposite direction out to sea by a gust of wind! I was too young to rant in those days and it is quite funny now.

TUESDAY 10TH JULY 2012

In the news today, we are propping up the failing Spanish economy by giving them £30billion. Personally I must have been asleep when I voted to give our tax payers money away to yet another foreign Country who are unable to balance their books.

Are we gullible or what. If you are aware of a foreign power that needs propping up because they are unable to get their own act together then just send a letter to 10 Downing Street and they will be only too happy to give you a wad of money for them. Oh by the way the government would also have no hesitation in raising tax on petrol or raising the level of VAT to extract more funds from you.

They already extract blood from you by slapping a tax on your hot pasty, what next? I am sure they will not disappoint me with the next stupid idea. Can you imagine those highly paid civil servants in a brain storming session, flip charts and pens at the ready!

"We need to raise more revenue, what have we not taxed to the hilt?"

"We already tax wages, tax savings and tax pensions. We pretend to give money to the NHS by taxing the workers again and calling it NI"

"We slap hefty VAT on everything you can think of, especially the people's favourite's tobacco and alcohol." "Think, think there must be something we have missed!" "At this rate we will be taxing the air we breathe and having sex!"

"That's it!, we will slap a tax on breathing air, after all water is not free just because it comes out of the sky, so neither is air. Work out how much individuals use put a price on it and VAT at 20%, job done. Now sex, easy, how many times a year would the ordinary person have sex, work it out and again come up with a figure and slap a 20% tax on it. Individuals who admit to having more sex than the norm put them in the 40% bracket for being cocky!"

WEDNESDAY 11TH JULY 2012

Well Spain has introduced its austerity measures increasing the retail tax from 18% to 21% as well as slashing the social care costs. Welcome to the real world. For the ex-pats the news is the house market has slumped by 25%, well that is the end of the good life, oh and the euro is worth 78 pence. Can't come back to UK though not enough houses to go around!

The bum fight is on to reform and modernise the House of Lords, oh here we go again. Good value for money though it will only cost the tax payer £25 million to do it, and I am not one to predict, but we will most likely end up with a load of yahoos who are just there to feather their own nest.

They will be elected of course but hey if you have a load of friends and good networking you could get elected to anywhere if you wished. Just look at the recently elected City Mayors!!! No, call me an old fuddy duddy but the old boys in their ermine have done an OK job and are supposedly neutral. If you looked back at the challenges and amendments to Bills they have certainly ruffled some Conservative and Labour feathers.

Seafordsurf Radio is going from strength to strength and we are always on the lookout for new talent to join the team of presenters. Chris Moyle's is free at the moment and we are awaiting his call. As you transmit from a place of your choosing you can be anywhere in the world. If you get time also visit www.projectoneyearon.co.uk which is one site created by Seafordsurf Designs.

Update 1: Due to valued feedback from our customers, in January 2013 Seafordsurf Designs reverted to its original name Frogbeat co.uk. This actually proves a point that we do not need to reorganise and rename established institutions such as the NHS and Primary care trusts. Leave it alone and let the people who care run the services as they should be run.

THURSDAY 12TH JULY 2012

Good morning world and a big thank you to the hackers who stuck a mother of a virus on my computer last night. Very clever indeed you bits of scum. It was a ransom ware virus "pay us £100 and we will unfreeze your computer". Yer right I am sure you would as well. Do you think I am that stupid to pay you for attacking my computer? Go and crawl under the stone from where you were born scumbag!

Watch out for these scams, do not pay up and just as important make sure your virus protection is up to date. But a word of warning my BT protection was up to date and the virus got through. It may pay to install a free one as well, like AVG.

Also be ready to download a Trojan killer like Trojan killer 2.1 which is currently on the market.

Anyway to business! If you are visiting Seaford and feel hungry then pop into the Seafordsurf Kitchens at the British Legion. Great homemade grub at affordable prices, you cannot get better than that.

The kitchens which is a new venture by the team at Seafordsurf Radio has become very popular with the local community and visitors alike.

Update 1: A Seaford Surf kitchen, as a business, was extremely successful and went from strength to strength. The menu was variable, the food excellent quality with a good price which was ideal for the clientele in the British Legion Seaford. Due to influences within and restrictions on ideas sadly the kitchens shut its doors in early August 2012. I would like to personally thank Russell and Colette on their Business venture, you worked so hard and it was a great success. Well done.

FRIDAY 13TH JULY 2012

Well here we are again on Friday 13th. Remember not to walk under any ladders, wear your lucky pants and if you spill the salt throw some over your shoulder.

For those who are eagerly waiting for the publication of "Chooooon the pictorial journey of internet radio station Seaford Surf" the wait may not be too long now. Yet another revision has been submitted to the publishers only ten minutes ago.

There have been potential problems with copyright over some of the images hence a rewrite and new images to be uploaded. We are now at a stage where the manuscript will be scrutinised, before publication can take place. Now, I do not have any issues with copyright as I do not wish to have any of my material used without my consent.

However I do have to ask the question how do the national press and other publications get away with "editing" images of celebrities by putting different heads on bodies for instance and nobody complains about it. It is just a different world sometimes, as indicated in an earlier blog!

SATURDAY 14TH JULY 2012

I am humbled, truly humbled. We moan and we groan. We complain if there is a queue at the supermarket and we get V signs if we don't drive fast enough for the tailgaters. We are getting more impatient with each other. Why?

If I could answer that I would be worth a £million! It is not until we step back and take a moment that we realise how foolish it is! I met a representative and children of Heltwate School Bretton yesterday and I was brought down to earth. The school deals with the education of children from 4-16 who are in the category of special needs.

One young girl maybe about 14 stood behind her wheel chair to ask for items to help fund the school, clothes, pens, pencils, books and anything else which they could use to assist fund the school. She was so sweet and she was so tired standing and refused to sit down as she was determined to do her bit with the teacher. I am determined to do my bit for these youngsters at the school. Watch this space for updates. A very humbled DJ Wayne

SUNDAY 15TH JULY 2012

Here is a question for you:

What do you do with a stack of video cassettes which have been in the loft because someday you may wish to view them? Now there are a number of issues here of course! One being that the last video recorder we had in our house was over five years ago! So why are the cassettes still in the loft?

At one time they went to the nearest charity shop, but now they even refuse to take them. There must be millions of these things in lofts, basements, garages and storage boxes.

There is only one solution! The waste bins and then landfill. It is unbelievable to know that future generations and indeed the third world will not even of heard about video cassettes, perhaps that may be a good thing. VHS or Betamax? Now, that was great debate in its day. What a waste of time that turned out to be. If you are able to answer the question you may stumble on a fortune, please remember me when you do.

MONDAY 16TH JULY 2012

News today: that there will be a huge investment into the rail system which will benefit all passengers. Well let me rephrase that.

The investment will probably be one selected line on the network and the downtrodden passengers who have had to stand all the time will be told the price of a season ticket has exploded by 15% to pay for the improvements.

I still say that Dr Beeching was the worst thing that ever happened to this Country and I firmly believe he was a naive infiltrator with the remit for bringing the rail network to its knees.

In that respect he did a great job. If the branch lines had not been decimated we would have a very credible rail network going into Towns and villages which have grown and grown with the population trend of moving out of Cities. As it stands many villages do not have a rail connection or a bus service.

TUESDAY 17TH JULY 2012

Monday night's Blues show which featured the top 100 blues tunes of all time which influenced musicians and artists ended in a cracker.

There was Gary Moore with "As the years go passing by" and then at number 100 Buddy Guy with Stone Crazy. Nothing could be better than that. So how can that be followed?

Well after much soul searching from next Monday we will be playing the best selling Blues songs of all time commencing with 100 Last kiss - Joe Bonamassa. This show is going to be so good. Please do not miss it.

The SSR bash is not far off and the weather is improving for the campers among us (not DJ Wayne & Mrs DJ Wayne). Rumour has it that the Weirdbeard family have booked into a campsite close to Seaford and Potty mouth Shed will be joining them.

As mentioned on Monday nights show items to take with me include one English Schilling, Bag with £9 4s 2d, Cap, purse and two further items? All will be revealed very soon.

WEDNESDAY 18TH JULY 2012

I wonder sometimes, why individuals get angry. Why is it that some people actually thrive on being miserable and inflicting that misery on others.

A prime example of course is the so called drivers of vehicles who seem to tailgate the vehicle in front in order for them to go faster, over the speed limit. It was on the news today that the death rate on British roads has risen for the first time in 10 years.

Opposition party labour rant that it is the Governments fault! Don't talk twaddle it is the idiots on the road who disregard the speed limits and intimidate other road users.

The other example is retail customers who go into the shops with the intention of being an ass shouting and screaming in order to get a discount, a replacement product, or to be a downright numpty!

This, I believe, is a product of current television and advertising. The methods advertising companies use, and how they portray their products is "must have" and "affordable"

What gives them the right to tell me I must have the product and how the hell can they tell me I can afford it anyway. That is probably why loan sharks and debt collectors are doing so well these days!

Thank goodness for SSR! Chill out mix with the best in the business, have fun, enjoy life as it should be enjoyed. You can tell I am off to Yoga with Cheryl and Mrs DJ Wayne tonight for a good wind down session and then off to the local boozer for a wind up session

THURSDAY 19TH JULY 2012

Weirdbeard has stories to tell which may well get you ranting. Like the asylum seeker who raped a girl of 12, got 3 years (you can get that for theft) disgusting, but could not be deported to Sudan as it may be against his human rights.

As Si said we are really in safe hands with these "numpties" running the legal system. Is it time they retired for the good of the country? Tell you what SSR DJs can do a better job, and get it right, we could not do a worse job!

For a start stop any social security payments, housing benefits, and tax credits payouts for them their partners, ten kids and cousin's dogs and cats!

If a guest in this country commits a crime, robbery, rape, murder, picking their nose, SEND THEM BACK TO WHERE THEY CAME FROM! Let their own kind deal with them. Tough on them if they don't like it, what is right is justice!

FRIDAY 20TH JULY 2012

What the hell 1?

The government is paying a company to wake teenagers up in an effort to get them back to work! Young people will also be driven to interviews and helped to get in to the habit of "turning up on time" to jobs. The government is just as weak as some of the mamby pamby wishy washy mummy boys and girls we are producing in this country. Bearing in mind the company is paid for out of taxpayers' money.

I for one, demand, that my contribution towards this scheme is stopped right now and put to better use. The country is in debt and we are taxed to the hilt, and for what, so some individuals can go on a jolly in their jim jams. Perhaps they will be the next generation of MPs in parliament?

What the hell 2?

News that some rail workers will strike the night before the Olympics' starts turns my stomach. Thanks for nothing for being proud of the British achievements and ensuring you serve the visiting public with pride!

What the hell 3?

News just out that some public servants will strike during the Olympics over "terms and conditions" this will affect travellers who may have to wait up to 4 hours to get in to the country. The solution is easy if they do not want to work then leave the job and recruit those who wish to work (discounting the lazy jim jam wearers who are unable to get their ass out of bed and turn up for an interview on time)

Have a great day!

SATURDAY 21ST JULY 2012

One of the favourite pastimes ever is meandering across a sandy beach, dodging the dog poo, and finding items of interest. A colourful shell, an odd shaped pebble, pieces of interesting driftwood and of course whale vomit, which is what one person found on the beach in Morecambe.

Apparently whale vomit, also known as ambergris is very valuable and is an ingredient in perfume. The 6 pound lump of smelly spew could be worth in the region of £50,000. So the next time you feel sick, after a night out on the booze followed by a kebab, chips, pickled onion and a pickled egg, send a lump off to be analysed, you just never know?

SUNDAY 22ND JULY 2012

Well done to Bradley Wiggins the first British rider to win the Tour de France (Tour of France to you and me) it was a fantastic display from the Brit, especially with the lead up to the Olympics. Even better it was a Team effort; let's see more of that in the forthcoming weeks.

Even better of course was the Weirdbeard Sunday slowdown on Seafordsurf Radio this evening. The playlist was excellent. Thanks Rock God. Si will be back on Thursday with the weekly Rock show.

MONDAY 23RD JULY 2012

In the news today Iraq bombings kill 91 people. Syria is imploding with a civil war that will kill thousands and all the UN can do is sit back on their haunches and watch.

Oh I forgot they can write another memo on a scrappy bit of paper deploring the situation. Britain "watch out" do not get embroiled in yet another futile war that nobody can win.

Let the Arab States sort out their own mess. They will only turn against us afterwards anyway, after we have taken in 100,000 refugees and re-housed them.

Sounds harsh I know but history speaks for itself. I feel for the people and cry for them but it is far too big for a small country like the UK to sort out. The Arab league is there for that purpose.

If only Mutton Geoff and Knobby could put on a concert for them they would forget about bombing each other. All it takes is a "whole lotta knobby".

More news: Day 66 of the Olympic torch relay Lewisham to Wandsworth, and Chris Hoy will be the flag bearer for Team GB. Congratulations Chris.

Update 1: Saturday 26th January 2013 the UK government "gives" Syria another £21.5m towards their refugee crisis. The total now stands at £89.5m. Has the situation improved? I think that may be a resounding no! That money would be better spent on the people who put it in the pot via VAT, NI and Income tax.

TUESDAY 24TH JULY 2012

Well, there are only four days to go before the biggest event in British history. No not the Olympic Games, I mean the Seafordsurf Bash 2012. All the resident DJs will be there for the autograph and book signing during the evening. Book signing? Oh yes the official release of Chooooon the history of internet radio SSR in pictures including the Frogbeat ultimate quiz.

During the evening there will be an auction of the very first American edition which has pictures which have been deleted in the UK due to copyright issues. Welcome to Nutsville will be performing live during the evening. There will be presentations, a monologue or two and the ultimate pantomime ever!

WEDNESDAY 25TH JULY 2012

Great day today, finished work at lunchtime, shopping (ok not that great) Yoga, pub and then food. Ah it is great to be English (that is why half the world wants to come here!!!

Anyway not long to go now before the SSR Summer Bash. Everybody is welcome. Come along to the rugby Club in Seaford. Welcome to Nutsville will be playing. There is entertainment with the resident DJs then a Book Signing with DJ Wayne. Oh and not forgetting the Health & Safety sketch.

THURSDAY 26TH JULY 2012

Itinerary for today:
Dogs in to kennels √
Breakfast √
Travel down to Seaford √
Lunch at the British Legion √
Geocache √
Book in to Hotel √
Geocache √
Evening at the British Legion √
Hotel & Good night √
See you there

FRIDAY 27TH JULY 2012

Travelled from Peterborough to Eastbourne via London, that was the wrong thing to do. Due to congestion on the M25 we changed the GPS to avoid motorways. This meant we went via the outskirts of London. WRONG THING TO DO! Olympic lanes and congestion charge what on earth is going on? Don't get me wrong I love the Olympics so Olympic lanes OK. However the London congestion charge is £15 for passing through. What a rip off. Boris you should be ashamed of yourself! It is disgusting and immoral. It is just another tax for the sake of having a tax. Should bump up the coffers for the Mayors Ball I suppose!

Eastbourne - now Eastbourne is a lovely place but you have to pay a tax to breathe. Every car parking space has a pay meter. The Hotel has no spaces so finding space is a challenge even before the money goes in to the machines. RIP OFF. The SSR bash is Saturday and the entertainment is finally coming together. However the despatch company who were supposed to get a package to Seaford by today failed in their task. It did not arrive!!!!!!!!!!

SATURDAY 28TH JULY 2012

The final preparations are well under way for the SSR bash tonight at the Rugby club in Seaford. At the meeting this afternoon, held at the British Legion, all the DJs were present to go through the final running order for the evening.

Welcome to Nutsville will start. During the break there will be comedy entertainment with DJ Wayne and the SSR DJs. They will be performing a monologue interpretation of Stanley Holloways "Albert and the lion." Then it will be "Kiss me quick" with Vanburger and DJ Wayne.

Welcome to Nutsville will finish the evening off. There will also be a book auction in aide of Help the Heroes. This is not to be missed!!!!!!! Other surprises as well. Watch this space for details

SUNDAY 29TH JULY 2012

The day after the night before! The SSR Summer bash exceeded expectations. The entertainment was provided by the fantastic "Welcome to Nutsville" who played two superb sets.

The above pictures are stills from the SSR Bash video which can be found on You Tube

The second sketch was with DJ Wayne and Vanburger and focused on Health & Safety in the Navy. Specifically, Vice Admiral The Right Honourable The Viscount Nelson KB and Vice Admiral Sir Thomas Masterman Hardy 1st Baronet GCB. There were queues for the book signing and it was a good thing there was security there to control the crowds as they surged forward. Both recordings are available to be viewed and enjoyed on You Tube.

MONDAY 30TH JULY 2012

A friend of mine drove through a reputable drive through and got to the window and ordered. "That will be £4.25p" said the young cashier. I handed over a £5 note and 25p. The cashier said, "You gave me too much money". I replied, "Yes I know but this way you just give me a £1 coin back". The cashier sighed and went to get the Manager who asked me to repeat my request, which I did. He handed me back the 25p saying, "We are sorry but we do not do that sort of thing". The cashier then proceeded to give me back 75p in change. Easy to confuse! Maybe but I believe there is an educational issue here!

TUESDAY 31ST JULY 2012

Last night's show continued with the top 100 bestselling blues tunes of all time and what a list it was! The feature "On this day" was informative, very cultured is DJ Wayne!!. The new feature "SSR Geocache" went down a storm. For those who are unaware of geocaching, basically it is similar to a treasure hunt, using your GPS.

The very first SSR Cache was placed in or around the village of Turves but not just a simple cache, oh no. There were two optional parts. The first one is to take a photo of a passing train at the crossing and then post it on line (no not the rail line!) The second optional challenge was to join the SSR listeners on the DJ Wayne show and confirm success.

Hot news off the press - the SSR resident DJs are making their way home from the four corners of the world (strange that, as the world is supposedly round) anyway normal DJ activity will be resumed very shortly. Oh and Team GB are in the medals, how cool is that. My Union flag (not allowed to say Union Jack it may upset the other Nations who are included) is flying proudly from my bedroom window.

WEDNESDAY 1ST AUGUST 2012

Telephone conversation:

Bank: how can I help you?

Me: I want to change the date of a Direct Debit

Bank: certainly account number?

Me: 1234567

Bank: Are you the account holder?

Me: No it is in Mrs DJ Wayne's name

Bank: Can I speak to her?

Me: No she is at work

Bank: In that case I can't discuss due to Data protection

Me: I have the details it is a joint account

Bank: I cannot give you the information

Me: I have the information; I will give it to you

Bank: Sorry I am unable to provide you with the information

Me: Not getting this are you. I have the details in front of me and I will give the information to you.

Bank: data protection I cannot tell you

Me: You don't need to tell me, I will tell you.

Bank: I need to speak to Mrs DJ Wayne

Me: She is not here and I have all the details you will ever need

Bank: I am terminating this call

Me: $%£&&*^ *^$%^* * up your backside you %^I*^$$ arrogant %^&$£ upstart what if my wife was here and unable to speak what would you do then?
....silence

Data Protection! Only when it suits!!!

THURSDAY 2ND AUGUST 2012

Team GB Team GB Team GB Team GB Team GB Team GB. Come On! How proud do you feel? It just gets better and better. You have to ask the burning question why Scotland would wish to break away from a great partnership. Throughout history, apart from a few battles, we have stuck together and died together. The thin red line is a part of history which should never been forgotten.

I remember when I first joined the British Army, yes the British Army, and one of the very first scary Scot I met was in the stores. A warrant Officer in the Argyll and Sutherland Highlanders so proud so dignified and yet a gentleman. He was disgusted at the amalgamation and decline of one of the very best regiments in the British Army. Formed in 1881 they fought many battles and fought at El-Alamein. They gave their lives for Britain, and for what?

In 2012 this government, in their defence review have virtually disbanded this heroic regiment and deemed it fit for ceremonial duties. Why? To save money so we can send it abroad to the very people we fought for world freedom. Well, I have answered my question then. You can understand how the Scots really feel. However let's stick together and line up against the real enemy.

I do come back to a question in a recent blog. "How do we know that members of this government are not out to destroy what is good about this union? After all famous spies have come out of Oxford and Cambridge!!!!! This is DJ Wayne and hey what great Country we have, and as Canned Heat said "Let's stick together"

FRIDAY 3RD AUGUST 2012

One recuring theme of this blog is fly tippers and those individuals who leave their litter where they choose and could not give a damn about their actions and the effect it has on others, as well as the environment in which we all have a responsibility to protect. There have always been those individuals who just disgard their unwanted pieces of litter anywhere they like without a moments thought or regret. I believe, since the introduction of new charges and raising others, the fly tipping situation has become much worse. Unscrupulous individuals will not pay to discard their unwanted rubbish they will illegally dispose of it elsewhere. The photograph below was taken whilst out walking on a Sunday aftenoon across the Fens near Peterborough.

The dump which included building waste and asbestos was adjacent to a small stream which flowed to a field where horses were grazing. The asbestos poisoning will do them the world of good! The individuals responsible are scumbags of the first ilk and when caught must be prosecuted without any hesitation.

SATURDAY 4TH AUGUST 2012

Whilst out walking I often wonder what the surroundings would have looked like years ago before fields were replaced by roads and houses, by digging up the green lands to be replaced by concrete, bricks and tarmac.

Even walking through the towns and villages I wonder what the surroundings may have looked like before houses were pulled down to be replaced by supposedly modern architecture. Then there are the houses where residents have moved out to be replaced by others who have a different idea about the internal and external décor. I wonder what happened to planning permission in these instances.

The previous picture is a prime example of seeing blue. The resident obviously had a job lot from "Del Boy". Admittedly this is not the worst example I have come across, but close your eyes and imagine the row of terraced houses as they used to be. The same brick work, roofs with slate tiles, no external dishes, cumbersome wheelie dishes, broken down front garden walls and unkempt gardens.

When did it all start? When did we stop believing in ourselves? When was it deemed unimportant? When did we become dishevelled and have this couldn't care less attitude to ourselves?

SUNDAY 5TH AUGUST 2012

Now I have a bit of a dichotomy here. I was out geocaching today, around Peterborough, and stumbled across some paintings on a side wall in an underpass in Fletton. The question is street art or graffiti. I have often ranted, on SSR, about mindless yobs that spray paint all over the place and just disregard the impact on society as a whole. I have no time for them and hope one day they have paint daubed all over their houses and cars.

However this is different. These paintings are superb and have the local council authority backing to be artistic at certain locations within the city. The artists themselves are full of talent and get a kick from seeing their paintings in public. It is far better to embrace these talented individuals than drive them out as the backlash would be graffiti everywhere and that would be horrendous.

Street art at its very best please enjoy.

MONDAY 6TH AUGUST 2012

What a great day for Team GB again, you cannot help but feel that tingle down your spine. Here is another tingle. Street artist "Nycee" at is very best.

Street Art by Nyces in Peterborough

Street art by Carl in Peterborough UK
Follow Nyces from the link on www.projectoneyearon.co.uk

TUESDAY 7TH AUGUST 2012

Whilst out geocaching on Sunday we wandered through Bretton just outside Peterborough, We past a block of new houses and flats that were very near to completion. Some had already been occupied by families who were probably living the dream of moving in to a new home. I was truly shocked to see a poster in the windows advertising the houses for sale, 95% mortgages available or shared ownership. Nothing wrong with that I hear you say! Well, the thing is they were all in Polish, Ukrainian, Iraqi and Afghanistan languages. Now, we are always being told that we need thousands of new houses so we build on green land and flood plains. So why are we building houses for foreign speaking Nationals? It is absolutely disgusting that we seem to be building new properties for refugees and not families on Council waiting lists. It is about time the Government listened and did something about it! Right Now!!

WEDNESDAY 8TH AUGUST 2012

In the news last night a number of magistrates court cases in Peterborough have had to be cancelled or delayed because of a lack of interpreters. It seems that the official interpreters do not like the fact that the company they work for is being privatised. Now, there are a number of issues here. Firstly if you do not want to work for the company and carry out your scheduled responsibilities then there is always the option to leave! Let others work who wish to work! Then there is the issue of the court case itself. Why do we need interpreters in the first place? Because the defendant cannot speak or understand English! Question: How do they interact with their solicitors then? And if they do interact with their solicitors why can't the solicitors be the interpreter???? It gets worse: The defendant does not speak English so odds on they are a guest or an illegal in this country. Why are we messing about? Send them back to the country they came from, stop wasting tax payer's money and that will stop them allegedly committing a crime! Something has got to be done NOW!

THURSDAY 9TH AUGUST 2012

A post box painted gold in a Teesside town in honour of Olympic champion rower Kat Copeland has been vandalised. Cleveland Police said that the damage to the post box, in Ingleby Barwick, near Stockton, consisted of initials scratched into the paintwork. They said two girls from outside the area were thought to be responsible and they were arranging to speak to them.

It came after a gold post box in honour of fellow gold medal winner Jessica Ennis was vandalised in Sheffield. The graffiti on the box in Sheffield read "Go Jess". Fans are also thought to have picked gold flecks from Andy Murray's post box in Dunblane as mementoes. Copeland and rowing partner Sophie Hosking won the women's double sculls on Saturday. Cleveland Police said: "We were made aware of the Olympic gold post box" Sometimes, just sometimes I am lost for words!

A golden opportunity indeed, for me to pose for the camera outside Doddinton post office Cambridgeshire, where they proudly celebrate the success of Jonnie Peacock, who won a Paralympics gold medal in the 100 metres.

FRIDAY 10TH AUGUST 2012

Well, the weekend is nearly upon us once again and only four days remain in the Olympics. Team GB & NI have done a fantastic job, a great show and what lovely athletes they have been. They fought hard to win competitions and have been gracious in defeat. True sportsmen and sportswomen! So why of why did one columnist in the UK national press write about the Olympics as being old fashioned and a waste of time and tax payers' money. What an idiot! He also stated that performing and competing for a first prize was not to be proud of and indeed competing against each other should not be allowed. What a double idiot and a prat. The newspaper in question should ditch this idiot and get someone in who can write common sense not dribble and rubbish. DJ Wayne is available and willing to take over the slot! Just email me at **wayne@whittleseasurf.com** and I can start tomorrow I certainly will not do any worse.

SATURDAY 11TH AUGUST 2012

It always amazes me how awful some people can be. I have on many occasions stated that human beings are basically ill mannered and downright rude. It is getting worse, probably due to the influences of TV and advertising. Vehicle drivers cut you up or pressurise you in to increasing your speed, shoppers in retail outlets are short tempered and are so demanding trying to get discounts or items for free. If they do not get it they start ranting and shouting at the poor retail assistant. So it may not be surprising that a lovely restaurant has decided to call it a day due to disagreements with the owners of the establishment. Customers should not shout, swear and be damn rude when requesting their food just because they are regulars at the venue. They are outdated and pathetic. Give up your running of the club to people with vision and modern ideas or you will not be in existence in this competitive environment. It is your bloody loss you old farts.

Update: Seafordsurf kitchens closed its doors for the last time in August 2012. Although the venture was a complete success there were certain elements which made it impossible to carry on. There is no need to be impolite to anybody and we all deserve to be respected although points of view may differ at times. I find it abhorrent that individuals can behave so poorly; they are an embarrassment to themselves!

SUNDAY 12TH AUGUST 2012

The opening ceremony was great, 29 Gold, 17 Silver, 19 Bronze. The closing ceremony was even better. Congratulations to everyone involved and that means all the thousands including the wonderful volunteers who did it for the love. I salute all and every one of you....thank you.

Only one thing why so much French, after all they admit they refuse to speak English at any event in France! Whatever! Now the fantastic games have finished listen and watch out for the political fallout and leaches who will now cash in their bonds. Watch this space for details in the coming weeks and months. One good thing, as we look forward to Rio, we know there will be some great dancing from some lovely ladies! I love sport, bring it on!

MONDAY 13TH AUGUST 2012

Have you noticed anything different about your local Methodist church? No? Well the first observation is “Is it there”? In the space of one week I have read that a number of churches have been totally demolished, no doubt to make way for a grotesque housing estate, another blot on the landscape. Then there is the Methodist church which sits on North Green in the village of Coates. This quaint old church which is over 170 years old, and recently renovated, held its very last sermon on Sunday 12th August 2012. Why? Well if you know then please share that with me. God forbid it is to be demolished and houses and flats erected in its place. It is in wonderful surroundings and is an ideal venue for the locals to use. Is this going to be yet another venue boarded up and left to rot, like many others? Come on you local authority. Do something about it now, before the rot sets in. That is what your job is all about. Prove your jobsworth!

TUESDAY 14TH AUGUST 2012

Again, if you missed it try to catch the broadcast in the afternoon on SSR. A great story in the press Matthew Onyskiw told his colleagues at work he would run naked through the streets of Peterborough if POSH (Peterborough Utd) did not get relegated in the 2011/2012 season. Well low and behold POSH did manage to stay up and his colleagues reminded him of his rant. So, true to his word he said he would do it, only if his work colleagues contributed to Thorpe Hall Hospice. An amazing sum of £930 was raised so off he went. However so save all four of his cheeks going red with embarrassment he was allowed to wear a mankini. Now have you seen Borat in his mankini? This is so funny as Matthew is pictured wearing a green one with a jock strap underneath. Double protection indeed!

WEDNESDAY 15TH AUGUST 2012

Well at 7am this morning it was confirmed that Virgin will lose the West coast franchise and will be replaced by First Group. How strange, but stay with me and I will point out the reasons why. Virgin has done an excellent job since they took over the franchise, introducing new rolling stock and making considerable improvements. First Group, they say, will "offer substantial improvements in the quality and frequency of services." Unions and rail campaigners have argued "jobs will be cut, fares and catering services will be cut back" Personally I believe it will be the latter!

As part of the flawed deal First Group will pay the Government £5.5bn over the franchise term, which runs until 2026. Why? This money goes into the Government coffers to be lost. This money could be put back into the Rail Network to provide an affordable travel for everyone. Crazy indeed! Oh by the way from January 2013 rail fares will increase by 6.2% by using an outdated formula which has no bearing whatsoever on transport and in particular rail costs. Come on Ministry of Transport pull your finger out, get a grip of reality and start working as the Ministry of Transport instead of working out stupid schemes to work out where the next buck is coming from. Keep your noses out of it and do what you do well, having garden parties, fat cat jollies and free drinks at the bar.

Update 1. : Sir Richard Branson has challenged the franchise bid process and it is going to court to be discussed. Although there is little chance of Virgin keeping the franchise, now that the decision has been made, it may change the way future franchise bids are processed.

Update 2. Oh dear oh dear, as predicted by DJ Wayne the whole tender fiasco has now turned into a disaster which has seen £40 million down the drain. The government was tempted by unrealistic figures and greed and "lo and behold" their calculators were flawed as well! The whole process has been abandoned with some civil servants being suspended. Presumably they will be going back to school to swot up on their mathematics and calculator skills.

THURSDAY 16TH AUGUST 2012

Here is a news item I picked up on this morning. Apparently the FA says it has shut down more than 30,000 illegal Internet streams of its television matches last season. They argue there is a rapid rise in illegal live TV websites which come from foreign broadcasters TV coverage. Now I have to ask the question: Is anybody anywhere surprised to hear this is happening? It is so damned expensive to go to watch a live football match the ordinary working, or non-working, man has been pushed to one side. SKY BSB has again paid millions of pounds for the rights to broadcast Premier and league games so how can anyone who does not wish or cannot subscribe to SKY watch any football? The answer is illegal streams! I for one would have no qualms about googling "live football" to watch a match on my laptop. Would you? After all, watching it is NOT illegal, so pffft to the FA. A word in your "shell like" FA! How about stop paying these so called superstar football players thousands of pounds each week and start paying them what they are worth! That will save you millions of pounds for a start and then start charging a fair price at the turnstiles. This way the true football fan will return to watch live the national sport of football!

FRIDAY 17TH AUGUST 2012

After the fantastic success of "Whittlesea's Got Talent" in March 2012 the Internet radio SSR in conjunction with Whittleseasurf is promoting "Whittlesey Talent Show 2012" All Bands, groups and individual singers are encouraged to enter the show which will take place on selected dates in October and November 2012. The venue will again be "Quinn's Place" Whittlesey. Entry forms are available from wayne@whittleseasurf.com

Update 1: The Talent show was a phenomenal and outgrew all our expectations. The final night was superb and any of the finalists could have been crowned winners. After much deliberation the eventual winners were the young band "Amplified" who wowed the crowds with their ability to sing and play their musical instruments. Look out for them you will not be disappointed.

SATURDAY 18TH AUGUST 2012

Yesterday saw the official launch of the latest talent show produced by DJ Wayne in partnership with whittleseasurf, The Boat PH Whittlesey, Quinn's Place Whittlesey and Seafordsurf Radio.

DJ Wayne presents the first look of the banner for the all new "Whittlesey Talent Show" which is scheduled for October / November this year. We have confirmation the MC will be Ady from Laffingboymusic and one of the judges will be a well-known contestant from x factor.

Update 1: Promises promises, the well-known x factor contestant did not make it to the heats or the final show. In fact she did not even bother to inform us she would not be able to make it. Fame and fortune plays a part I suppose!

SUNDAY 19TH AUGUST 2012

Have you ever thought about jumping on to a bike again and setting off into the sunset, just like the heroes of those old movies? The sun is shining and what a beautiful day it will be today so why not? Well actually I could probably think of many reasons why not, and getting knackered is one of them! The thing is, with the Olympics now over, and I don't know if you have noticed but there seems to have been an explosion of cyclists taking to the roads, paths and trails, and I believe that is a good thing especially as levels of fitness with certain people may be an issue.

So, not wishing to be left out, Mrs DJ Wayne and myself purchased a couple of these two wheeled contraptions with a view to slinging them into the back of the car and going geocaching with them, perfect solution for the long routes we do. Now, I hear you say "two bikes in the back of a car?" Folding bikes is the answer! Ideal (or is it?) The thing is we intend to navigate around Rutland water on Sunday 26th, and you are very welcome to join us, but I am not too sure we will still be alive after the round trip of 17 miles or 26 miles if we navigate the peninsular route. So we have to rent a couple of bikes with a bigger wheel circumference to take a little of the pain away. Watch this space next week to learn how we got on

MONDAY 20TH AUGUST 2012

Geocaching yesterday was great although very hot with an embarrassing moment thrown in. We set out at 10.00 am which was a good time to start but it warmed up very quickly and two hours in, it was unbearable, and the route we were on was without any overhead cover. Mrs DJ Wayne had to resort to opening her umbrella for shade. Why did she take an umbrella? will come back to you on that one! Anyway we arrived at one site and there was a vehicle parked at the side of the road on the grass verge. We located the cache and noticed it had been signed previously by a geocacher we knew.

Now I and I don't know why assumed (starts with ASS) the man who was in the vehicle was him, so I gave him a good wave, and he waved back, so all well there. After I closed the cache, before we moved on, I said to Mrs DJ Wayne "just going to say hello before we move off", as I am polite like that! Anyway I walked up to the vehicle and said through the open window, "Hi how's it going then", He replied "Yep OK thanks you?" that was the pleasantries over with! I asked "how many you found today then?" Looking quizzically replied, "How many what?"

"Caches" I said.

"What" he replied? At this point I knew he was not the person I thought he was so had to think of an exit strategy.

"Ah", I began, "we are on a treasure hunt and thought you were as well",

"No, I stopped to send a text and have a cigarette", he said, now I had my exit.

"OK, well if you see anyone coming after us just tell them we went in the opposite direction, bye have a good day", and off I went with a skip and a jump, hopping past Mrs. DJ Wayne, who had gone on ahead and I soon caught up.

"Who was that?" she asked, "Not got a clue", I blurted, "stop faffing about and let's get going", and off we went. Well, I am sure there is a moral to this true story, and you will probably find it in my new book "Oh Blogger!" Have a good day - DJ Wayne

TUESDAY 21ST AUGUST 2012

Last night's show was the continuing story of the top 100 best selling Blues tracks ever and what some great tunes they were as well. It just gets better and better. To top that, if you were able, we had a local talent segment which featured songs by Marmite and the Pussyratz, Marcel and the Deltaphonics and Shelly Tickner. Marmite and Shelly were recorded live at Charters Peterborough. You can listen to Marmite's tracks on the Vanburger show. The tracks by Marcel were recorded in the studio, and I thought they were spot on. However I have just been informed they have been reworked in the studio and new versions will be available for playing on Monday nights Whittlesea scene and heard Blues Alchemy, really looking forward to that. If you did miss the Blues alchemy it will be available to listen to again after Vanburgers' drive time show.

WEDNESDAY 22ND AUGUST 2012

Great news, you heard it first here on DJ Wayne's blog and Seafordsurf Radio. After playing selected tracks by Marcel and the Deltaphonics on Monday nights edition of the Blues show the tracks are being remastered and a CD is being produced. But that is not all, the remixed tracks by Ade Pierce and Laffingboy music will be aired on the next Monday edition of Whittlesea Scene and heard, The Blues Alchemy. This is not to be missed, it is going to be awesome. Laffingboy music have a long history of producing quality music from their studios in Peterborough. So if you have a desire to record your own songs give Ade a call on 07906 649605 and mention DJ Wayne, won't get you a discount but it will make me happy. Or just follow the link from Whittleseasurf and contact him via his website, which will also have a link to Seafordsurf Radio. How is that for a great partnership?

THURSDAY 23RD AUGUST 2012

A friend's electric garage door had been playing up for some time now so they decided to bite the bullet and get a repairman in to sort it out. When he turned up and conducted the survey he informed them that they did not have a large enough motor to propel the door upward. This confused them as the door has the original motor still attached. It was the largest at the time being half horsepower. The repairman apparently shook his head and said, "Not big enough, you need quarter horsepower". They informed him that a half is larger than a quarter and he replied, "No no no, it's not, four is larger than two!" Needless to say they did not use this repairman.

FRIDAY 24TH AUGUST 2012

Well the Bank Holiday is upon us once again and quite rightly we are all looking forward to it, apart from those who have to work of course. Now I have had a rant on more than one occasion on my Monday night radio program, Bank Holidays are for Holidays! It seems nowadays it is an opportunity by the retail industry to make a fast buck and encourage us all to spend money which we do not really have. Individuals have fought and died for the right to take holidays and make the most of those precious times with their families. All that has now unfortunately changed as the retail industry convinces us all that it is we, the shopper, that has demanded longer opening hours and the convenience it brings. **WRONG:** The shopper will shop when the stores are open. The shopper will know they need to complete their shopping when the stores are open. The shopper is not stupid! Did we really have a problem when shops closed at 4pm and closed half day Wednesday, half day Saturday and closed on Sunday. NO, if you did not have your milk, bread or butter, you went without Tough!, but you soon learnt to plan ahead so it did not happen again. Come on everyone lets reverse this unsocial trend, spend leisure time with our families and you never know we may even get to know the neighbours, make friends and live in a truly happy world! Come on, we can do, the fat cats can get fat without our assistance!!!!

SATURDAY 25TH AUGUST 2012

At what point in our lives, or those before us did we start to become intolerant? Was it when we became able to own our own vehicles and become masters of our own destiny on the roads? The reason I ask is that drivers seem to be the most intolerant people in the universe. The majority seem to be miserable, offensive, ignorant and downright scumbags on the roads. In-courteous is an understatement. For example as I turned from a junction, which was on a bend. on to the main road a vehicle was just coming around the bend and started to speed up to get as close as possible to stick two fingers up at me. They just had to make a point. Why?

Why is it that now we have quality audio equipment in our vehicles we have to share the audio with the whole universe? The idiots follow you with "boom boom boom", they pass you on a dual carriageway with "boom boom boom". I came to a halt at a traffic light this afternoon and there was a guy washing his vehicle in his driveway and the car stereo was at full blast why? Bet he gets on with his neighbours! Anyway, today was the first outing on our fold up bikes, which fitted very comfortable in to the boot of our vehicle. We had chosen a flat route on the outskirts of Peterborough. Half an hour in the heavens opened up and we got totally soaked. Whose idea was that then?

SUNDAY 26TH AUGUST 2012

The Houses of Parliament may be up for a five year refurbishment plan costing an estimated £10bn over 10 years. I am sure the problem is not the mice which are reported to be having mice parties everywhere but the amount of hot air that comes from the main chamber which is damaging the structure of the ancient building!

Once in the chamber they seem to turn into werewolves sucking the life blood from opponents no matter what the discussion may be. I am very surprised the roof has not caved in earlier! Rumour has it the MPs may move out for the duration of the repairs maybe with a bit of luck half of them may not be able to move back, to be honest they may not be able to find their way out of a paper bag. They would however be able to find their way to the free bar and buffet!

As for the cost it may seem a lot of money but hey we seem to give that amount to the euro-zone every week so let's waste it on ourselves. Money well spent I say. We could of course spend it on the homeless (MPs) or the hungry (MPs) or the down and outs (err I will come to you on that one!) Tax payers for the taxpayer that's what I say!

MONDAY 27TH AUGUST 2012

Well, Bank Holiday in England and guess what the rain is threatening but hey that will not stop us from doing what we wish to do will it? After all we are not made of sugar are we? Mind you we did not manage to cycle around Rutland water on Sunday, after the trial with our fold up bikes on Saturday we decided to let the muscle strain heal up for a few days. How can bike riding hurt so much, after all it is only twenty years since I was last on one! Anyway the task today was to get on down to the allotment and do a little harvesting. Unfortunately a little bad news today, some of the sheds have been broken into and items have gone missing. Easy really as the locks are only a token and I guess if someone really wanted to steel items or cause havoc then it is not a difficult job.

All you would need is a crowbar. But that is not the point, if people steal food it is because they may be hungry so OK feed the kids. When items are stolen that is different in my eyes, they are scum. You try your best to grow a few veggies and some scumbags steel your fork and spade and smash windows and doors as well. No, I am sorry, scumbags, and I got a thorn in my finger and hit my thumb with my hammer, pity they did not take that as well I suppose!

TUESDAY 28TH AUGUST 2012

Do you get your tasks completed quickly or are you one of the many people who procrastinate until the very last minute. Apparently the percentage is high as the vast majority of us are happy to sit back twiddling our thumbs and put tasks off until another day. Don't read that nasty email, put letters to one side and hey we can mow the lawn tomorrow.

That is fine until the nasty email becomes mega important and must be read, the letter we put to one side is from the Inland Revenue and the lawn, well it has just been raining heavily for the last 48 hours Oh dear! Procrastination is a very lovely word but it can cause us a lot of bother!

WEDNESDAY 29TH AUGUST 2012

News item in The Peterborough Telegraph, "Whittlesey Dad DJ Wayne presents his books "Not so perfect cooking" and "Chooooon a pictorial journey with seafordsurf radio." Both available from Fast Print Publishing, reserve your copy now so you will not be disappointed!

THURSDAY 30TH AUGUST 2012

A world record has been set for a message in a bottle. A Scottish skipper found a message in a bottle after 98 years. The drift bottle, contained a postcard which promised a reward of six pence to the finder, was released in June 1914 as part of scientific experiment. You never know what is lurking about in the vast expanse of water which is surrounding us all. I remember back in the late sixties I was on a ferry between Harwich and the Hook of Holland which was a popular route, in those days, especially for military personnel, who were travelling between Europe and the UK. Did you notice "between Europe and the UK", ah happy days before the European parliament passed stupid laws enforcing Europe to all act the same way. How strange that the UK adopt the laws but other state members do their own thing.

Anyway whilst on this ferry with comrade in arms we had a great idea of putting messages in bottles and throwing them overboard thinking that they would be recovered quickly and we would make new friends. Now, of course the bottles containing vodka had to be emptied before the deed could be done, which was no problem. To this day I do not believe any of the bottles have been recovered and certainly to my knowledge nobody has collected the reward which was offered. Now, a point of order here! As copious amounts of alcohol was consumed the message may have mentioned a reward of £1million for the return of the bottle, this is now time expired of course!

FRIDAY 31ST AUGUST 2012

Have you noticed that we all seem to be suffering from nail fungus? Every five minutes on the TV adverts there is a person convincing me I have fungal disease so I keep looking at my mails and sure enough they could be right! I need to nip down to the pharmacy and pay my money for a product which will eradicate the disease and I will be happy again. Why did I not notice this earlier? Thank goodness for TV adverts and the media for keeping us all informed of this scourge so we do not have to keep our hands in our pockets just in case someone may see our devil fingers. Low and behold I am cured!!!!!

SATURDAY 1ST SEPTEMBER 2012

So Vanburger has arrived safely back from his excursion in Bavaria. Welcome home safe and sound and with lots of Bavarian lager. Sounds like he had a great time! Reminds me of when I was stationed there in the 60s seems like a million light years away now but if my memory serves me correctly I was there for a three month secondment. Not too sure what we were guarding, but sure it must have been important at the time, maybe a distillery or still or something! Anyway, we did our duty and the local community loved us. Funny really on every corner as you go in to the woods there is a huge wooden cross, obviously guarding you against the evils lurking within. Better safe than sorry, that's what I say!

SUNDAY 2ND SEPTEMBER 2012

As the sun was shining, we went geocaching today, around the wash at King's Lynn Norfolk, It is many years since I have been to "KL" so it was good to go back and have a nostalgic look around. We planned the geocache route to take in as many caches as possible, parked at the most convenient location and off we went. No bikes this time just Shanks's pony. It was all going well until our first

DNF then it became a bit of a chore. Not that we did not enjoy it but the walk took us through some very strange locations. Not sure if it was a footpath or an overgrown field. Trouble is after walking for five miles to the end of the estuary you are left with the walk back on the exactly the same route! So a pleasurable walk turned into a route march back to the car which we had parked in Kings Lynn.

MONDAY 3RD SEPTEMBER 2012

My brother lives in Sydney New South Wales and it is always interesting to hear strange stories from the outback. As you drive through the vast sprawling semi deserts there is always the danger of having an encounter with wild animals, namely kangaroos, wallabies or even wombats.

My brother recently had a new neighbour in the suburb he resides and she called the local council to request the removal of the "Wombat crossing" sign which was on the roadside near her house. When my brother asked why? She replied, "Too many wombats are hit by our cars out here, I don't think this is a good place for them to be crossing anymore!" Hey ho, life in the outback!

TUESDAY 4TH SEPTEMBER 2012

Doing your weekly shop in the supermarket is nothing but blight on mankind. For instance why do they not make the isles one way instead of creating trolley jams so the nerves get frayed and the ankles get bruised? And why do people have to be so dammed miserable as well? Ok it is not the best of activities to undertake but why do they have to go around with a face that looks like it has been hit with a frying pan and slouch over the trolleys as they push them around?

We have created a generation of miserable obese slovenly individuals with no sense of purpose in life. You can tell that when the kids, sorry lovely young children, scream and shout obscenities' because they want something to eat right now. So what do the parents do, tell them to be quiet and wait until they get home, no they grab a French stick or a bar of chocolate and shove it in their gobs to keep them quiet, until they get to the checkout.

Not all of them pay for the soiled goods of course; no they discard the half eaten merchandise on a shelf as they pass. That is really bringing up your children you pathetic stealing oiks!

WEDNESDAY 5TH SEPTEMBER 2012

Now I am all for individuals who wish to better themselves in this sometimes very cruel world. I fully understand that there may be a lack of employment opportunities in this current economic downturn. However there are numerous recruitment agencies out there that have a pool of people to be called upon when required. WRONG!

We required a replacement cleaner to cover holidays for one week and it has been an absolute nightmare trying to get a replacement. It seems to me that nobody actually wants to work for a living anymore. Now I come to the good part. The replacements we have had are unable to speak English. To communicate with them I have to turn into Basil Fawlty and speak pigeon English and wave my arms around like a demented person. Why should I need to do this? I hear myself speaking "you bin empty now rubbish there hoover yes understand hoover." Going well I thought! No response! "Bin yes empty e-m-p-t-y" ah well not essential, it can always wait until tomorrow. Let's try canteen, "hand towel, wipe clean yes?" oh dear this could be a long day, but not as long as yesterday when I had to let the other one go. This is a very small island and I suppose the land of opportunity but trust me we are getting in to a right muddle to say the least. Watch this space for the next update. DJ Wayne's blog does not hold back on what has to be said. What do you think? Have you experienced similar? Please let me know.

THURSDAY 6TH SEPTEMBER 2012

Interesting article in the Peterborough Telegraph today! Apparently there is an individual who resides in Turves who is very talented indeed. He is a noted author and respected member of the community. He has written, and had published not one but two books. He has also organised talent shows for the local community. He has had published "Not so perfect cooking" and "Chooooon a pictorial history of SSR part 1". Part 2 is being prepared right now. Hold on I can hear a trumpet........Oh it's me blowing it!!!! Hold on a minute I have just received a text: "Records show you may be entitled to a £2750 in compensation for miss selling of PPI on your credit cards and loans. Reply PPI for info or DECLINE to stop" Interesting as I have never had any PPI, and am sick to the back teeth in receiving these texts and emails. My reply: "Stop pi**ing me off you bunch of morons I have already text stop you pathetic bunch of time wasters and scourge of the community. You are at the same level as a pile of dog poo and fly tippers". Ah technology! Not had a reply yet!

Update 1: If you are receiving these very annoying texts on your mobile then forward those to *7726 (most networks) and your network operator will report it as SPAM.*

FRIDAY 7TH SEPTEMBER 2012

Ah the end of the week is finally here and what a week it seems to have been! Well the cleaner will be back on Monday and she will be so so busy! The replacements just did not work out. Are there any suitable people out there who would like to work for a living instead of claiming social security hand-outs, speak English and I do not mean pigeon English and do not stink! A tall order I know, but hey it could, maybe, be possible although do not hold your breath for too long, although I have been doing so this week.

SATURDAY 8TH SEPTEMBER 2012

London 2012 Paralympics it is one of those occasions that you just had to be there. I was there Sunday 8th September with Mrs D J Wayne and it was fantastic.

The travel, the people, the helpers and all the volunteers were the best of the best. The spirit of the games was beyond expectations.

I have nothing negative to say about anything, apart from the pint of lager (no proper beer on sale anywhere, how can that be?????) and half a cider costing more than my mortgage!!!!! Anyway hey ho enjoy the moment.

SUNDAY 9TH SEPTEMBER 2012

Sunday 9th September 2012 and the day was beautiful so Mrs DJ Wayne and myself made our way to the Whittlesey Festival which was a great day's entertainment full of music and dancing.

Some great local artists have signed up for the Whittlesey talent show it is going to be bigger than the X Factor (in my opinion). Entry is free. David Bailey & Kelly Oliver (pictured above right and Alice pictured above left) will be there!

MONDAY 10TH SEPTEMBER 2012

Back to reality! The Olympics and Paralympics have ended and many people will be coming down to earth with a bump. The focus has been on success and the ability to try as hard as possible to become the best of the best. The past month's events will certainly inspire a generation and we must not forget that. We must also not believe that everything will be better from now on. It will not.

The situation is the same as it was a month ago; broken Britain has had a plaster on to cover the wound but the cut is still there. Look around you, look up and down the high streets the problems are still as they were before. We are being taxed so much we will go the same way as the dodo and for what? To support the rest of Europe! There is no limit to immigration and the flood gates are open. How on earth are we supposed to support ourselves as well as the thousands of "Europeans" from Countries we never heard of ten years ago. STOP IT NOW! Instead of having a wet windy government it may be time for a change! Ponder on that until tomorrow!

TUESDAY 11TH SEPTEMBER 2012

If you go out walking the dog and he finds a bone or two do not forget to get it DNA tested, it could well be of archaeologist interest. In fact you yourself may very well go down in history as the individual who found a leg bone belonging to Bug Yang the terrible who was a warrior and became famous for terrorising women and children, plundering and looting villages and raping all the women and livestock! Or, you may have found the remains of Richard III the English King who perished at the battle of Bosworth in 1485. He was the last Yorkist king of England and died at the age of 32. His death ended the war of the roses. Apparently, archaeologists searching for the grave of Richard III have said "human remains found in Leicester show similarities to the king's portrayal in records." The remains found show signs of spinal abnormalities and a "cleaved-in skull" that suggest it could be Richard III,

Where were the remains found? Well, under a car park in Leicester of course! Mmm don't suppose the cleaved in skull happened when numerous vehicles have driven over it time and time again then, because that would certainly hurt my skull! Actually it is always interesting when remains like this are located. It is our history, it is English history, it is our heritage, lets enjoy the moment, before the Eurocrats in Brussels declare that Richard III never existed and there was never an England. Trust me that time will come The skeleton found beneath a Leicester car park was confirmed that of English king Richard III. Richard will be reinterred in Leicester Cathedral, or maybe York depending who wins the rights. Or is that last rights!

Update 1: According to the experts his skeleton had suffered 10 injuries, including eight to the skull, at around the time of death. Two of the skull wounds were potentially fatal. Richard was born at Fotheringhay Castle in Northamptonshire, where Mary Queen of Scots was later executed. As Duke of Gloucester, Richard took a rampant white boar as his sign. Richard is steeped in English history which should never be lost, and indeed passed on to our children and grand children. This is what this great island of ours is all about.

His coronation took place in Westminster Abbey, in a ceremony very similar to HM the Queen's. Richard had one of the shortest reigns in English history - 26 months and was the last English king to die in battle, killed by the forces of the future Henry VII. Other wounds included slashes or stabs to the face and the side of the head. There was also evidence of "humiliation" injuries, including a pelvic wound likely to have been caused by an upward thrust of a weapon, through the buttock. Well that's enough of that then, a bit like the in house fighting between the Conservatives and the Liberal Democrats.

WEDNESDAY 12TH SEPTEMBER 2012

Well it did not take very long then did it? As predicted in a previous blog UK and America have been drawn in to other people's battles and end up the bad guys themselves. I have said it time and time again let other Countries sort themselves out, why have we got to go and get involved, why have we got to be the saviours of the universe. How many forces personnel have given their lives in Iraq, Afghanistan and for Libya? For what? To be murdered by a terrorist wearing a police or army uniform. A so called blue on blue killing! They are not worth dying for. In Libya today a US official was murdered by militiamen who stormed the US consulate in the eastern Libyan city of Benghazi. Now if my memory serves me right these are the same people that the coalition forces assisted in getting rid of their dictator Colonel Gaddafi last year. They really appreciated that then. When will western governments learn the lesson, keep out of other people's business and leave them to their fate being ruled by an evil dictator. If they do not like it let them do something about it. British forces protect Britain not foreigners who will murder you when your backs are turned.

THURSDAY 13TH SEPTEMBER 2012

It is not very often that I agree with PMs and councillors as I firmly believe they only do good when there is something in it for them. My theory is water tight, just find out the names of individuals who are on your council planning committee. Most of them will be builders or associated with building! Anyway, interesting article in the Peterborough Telegraph today "MP will call on Parliament to close border due to "strain on resources." Thank goodness someone has the balls to stand up and be counted. Stewart Jackson MP for Peterborough has applied to present a controversial Bill on the matter to the House of Commons on Wednesday 31st October. He wants to change the "open border" policy between EU countries that has existed since 1985 because he feels Peterborough has become too crowded in recent years.

Good. I will be a little blunter; it is completely stupid to have open borders. No other country does it. We are the dumping ground for wasters and drop outs that cannot be employed in their own countries. The majority of those who come in are not employable and will be supported by the state, which they have not contributed to, for the rest of their lives. Not only that, the state will also have to support the rest of the relations as well. Farcical and stupid! 18.5% of the Population in Peterborough is now made up of recently arrived immigrants. As I have said in a previous blog only let in people who have a skill, have employment and have organised their own accommodation. I look forward to how the Bill will progress, but I will make a prediction now. It will not succeed because of the wet lettuce MPs and committee members in the House. They are scared to say and do what is right in case their free ticket in the bar is terminated. *I was right!*

FRIDAY 14TH SEPTEMBER 2012

I was talking with a colleague yesterday who lives in the sleepy village of Farcet situated in the heart of the Fens. Villages always give the impression of being close knit communities and this was no exception. The house he had moved in to was situated in a very nice part of the village in fact the purchase price also included owning a part of a road as well! As in most communities there are always the same few individuals who seem to be involved in fund raising and on committees organising fetes and car boots. My colleague took the opportunity to meet his neighbour who was one of these individuals who took part in organising these events. As well as organising events he also doubled as Santa Clause at Christmas time at the village hall, having done so for many years. He was also the village Mayor. My colleague was very impressed with the dexterity of his neighbour and would relay that message to his neighbour's wife who was not present at the moment. The following day he did see her going in to her property and took the opportunity to speak with her.

"Hello", he said

"Yes" she asked

"I'm your new neighbour just saying hello, I met your husband yesterday" he said.

"Oh did you" she answered.

"Yes and very impressed as well, he is involved in many activities in the village".

"Yes he is thank you" she answered again.

"And you must be a very lucky lady indeed?" he questioned.

"Yes and why is that?" she asked, puzzled.

"Well you may be the only lady in the village to be able to sleep with the mayor and Santa Clause every night of the week, a double act, so to speak?" he replied. Now, I don't know how that message came over but the Mayors wife was off the front step, in her house and the front door slammed shut. Needless to say there were no immediate intimate candlelight suppers to be had!

SATURDAY 15TH SEPTEMBER 2012

Why is it that when some people go out for a meal or a drink they believe they are allowed to be the messiest creatures on earth. It is noticeable wherever you go. Spilt drinks, rubbish and food left on tables and if any fall on the floor it is left there to be crushed into the carpet and floors. It is the same in the canteen where I work. Leftover food and drinks just left for someone else to tidy up. Water fountain overflowing because they could not be bothered to turn off the tap and the cup has overflowed. Dirty plates and eating utensils just left in the sink for someone else to wash up. It is absolutely disgusting. Are these people the same in their own houses? I wonder?

SUNDAY 16TH SEPTEMBER 2012

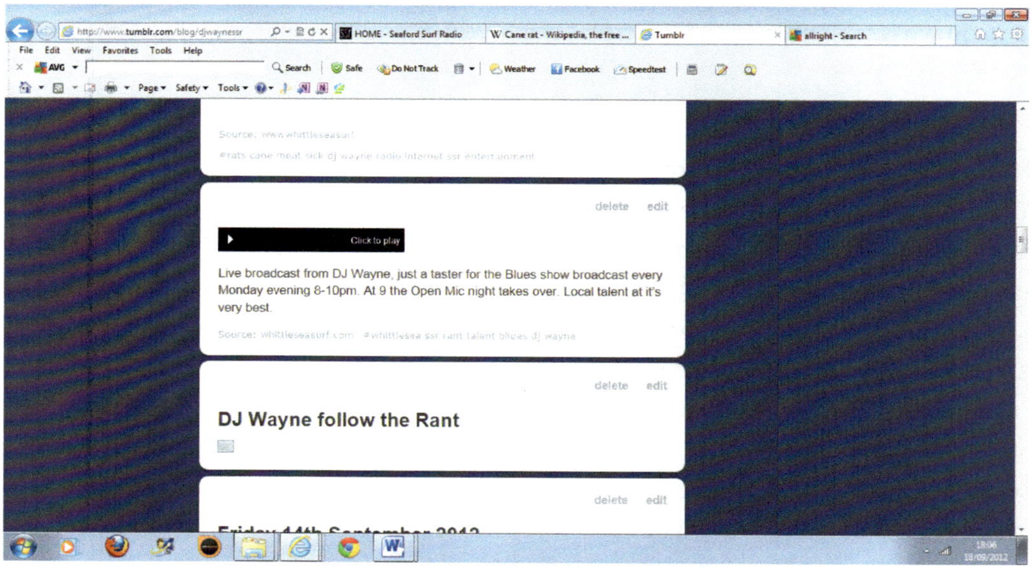

Ah the second broadcast on Spreaker by DJ Wayne

MONDAY 17TH SEPTEMBER 2012

I read with interest the article on the BBC news page today about cane rat meat being sold to the public in Ridley Road Market East London. Now, I don't know about you but even the thought of a rat alive or dead sends me in to palpatations. The only good rat is a dead rat and that is not for eating! Have you seen the size of these cane rats? They are massive! The practice of creating "smokies" is outlawed under UK and European food laws amid fears about public safety and animal welfare but that has not stopped a few butchers in London from trading in the illicit meat. It has also been linked to mafia-style gangs in Wales who steal sheep and goats, slaughtering them in unlicensed abattoirs*, and all this before the horse meat scandal!*

One Hackney butcher, who was secretly filmed, selling a BBC researcher quantities of the illicit meat, said: "Don't tell anyone, otherwise there will be trouble." Two African food stores have sold bush meat such as "grass cutter" or cane rats, which are described as having been imported from Ghana where they are a delicacy. Apparently the trade in bush meat is a persistent problem for the UK authorities with illegal meat products smuggled in by passengers in ferry terminals and airports. Am I missing something here? Are you telling me there is a growing market for this type of meat and if so, what is the reason? Is the ordinary person being priced out of the traditional meat dishes of chicken, pork and lamb? Not surprising if you have had a look at the prices in your local supermarket. I thought I was purchasing a whole lamb the other day but it was only for two chops and they had withered to the size of a fingernail after they had been grilled. Well I suppose there is only one answer to the growing cost of food! Give me a whole quality Cane rat anytime! Mmmmm yum yum yum and then pass the sick bowl!!!

TUESDAY 18TH SEPTEMBER 2012

I was looking in a long mirror today, not sure why, but I was and it reminded me of the occasion when I had to go to a well-known high street tailor to purchase a new suit for a forthcoming friend's wedding. It was one of those occasions when it just had to be done; there was no getting out of it this time. To look like a penguin you need to go to a penguin shop.

Now the shop assistant was very friendly, quite talkative and gave lots of advice. He advised me if the arms were too short or too long, the length of the legs and the all-important room around the nether region! There was also the colour to think about, should it be grey, black or a shade of brown! I was just not sure! Should I choose a square pattern, or stripes or even light spots which faded into the background? I was just not sure!

Should I choose wool mixed with polyester or perhaps the cotton may be a better choice? I was just not sure! I stood in front of the long mirror and turned from side to side. I walked up to the mirror and then walked back again. I hitched the waistband up and let it drop. I had the jacked open and then tried it with the buttons done up, one, two and three at a time. I was just not sure!

I did a little twirl, as you would when doing the chicken dance on the dance floor and turned to the assistant who was now chewing his non-existent nails, "I am still not sure, what do you think?" "Well Sir does look good", he answered, although not very convincingly. I looked in to the mirror one last time, "to be very honest", I said, "I look like a bag of sh*t, don't I?" "Sir, yes you do, you look completely like a bag of sh*t and I am unable to work any miracle with you today". And for a funny moment we both accepted the inevitable. "Right then" I said, wrap it up and I will take it now".

Thank you Sir, wise choice may I say, will 10% discount be alright?" "That will do nicely, good day, always a pleasure to do business with an honest man".

WEDNESDAY 19TH SEPTEMBER 2012

Ahoy matey, Ah ha me hearties, splice the main brace and issue the crew with a tot of rum. Today, September 19th is "Talk like a pirate day", so you had better join in or you will be keel hauled and whipped with a cat of nine tails! Oh arrrrr.

Swash buckle me hearties and get down to business. Pirate day is being celebrated all over the world with events organised in Cities, Towns, villages and hamlets and of course the centre of the internet universe Seaford. Swab the decks you landlubbers and get it all ship shape and Bristol fashion.

Avast me hearties, celebrations will be rife and no doubt pieces of eight will be changing hands or is that hooks? Get your best wooden leg out of the cupboard, dust it down, get rid of the woodworm and get ready for some hopping about on the dance floor. Look out for the Seaford shags who will be dressed as real pirates, smugglers and Saxons. Not too sure of the Saxons? Anyway be very aware of the skull and crossbones which could be raised up the flagpole today.

So Jim lad, all hands on deck and cor blimey get those scurvy dogs up in the crow's nest to look out for any man o war coming over the horizon. And if you don't oblige me you will be swinging from the yardarms listen to SSR **www.seafordsurfradio.com**. You have been warned! You may well walk the plank!

THURSDAY 20TH SEPTEMBER 2012

Isn't life funny and often very strange? If you visit your local Town but in particular the nearest City and you are walking down the paved area would you say "hello" to people, you do not know from Adam, who are walking by you? Would you even look then in the eyes and give them a wry smile? I believe the answer may be a resounding NO! For a start you may get a warning glance of "mind your own business, who are you looking at". It may be in some foreign tongue which you have never heard of. Not too sure if that is a good or bad thing of course. Don't know any potty mouth Shed words in any foreign language let alone one that ends in Stan!

How come there are so many Countries popping up which end in Stan? Who was this Stan? I believe him to be the marauding warrior I have spoken about before with all that raping and pillaging (not that I condone it) but there must have been a multitude of stans who then started their own empires! Anyway the point is if you did say hello to passers-by, you may well get a strange look or worse having six bells kicked out of you. So how come when you are on holiday in a different location, walking on the footpaths and bridleways you always ask the people coming towards you if they are OK? Don't get me wrong, I love it. I always ask "OK", "owdo", "how ya doing", or a resounding "Yo".

When asked if I am OK I will respond with a smile and a "Yep thanks great day", or a "thank you, do you listen to Vanburger on the drive time show on Seafordsurf Radio in the mornings and again on the drive time show in the evenings?" but that generally takes a little longer and by that time they have run across the grassy hill and out of site. Strange that, as it seems to happen quite a lot!

Anyway being in another location always seems to bring out the best in people. This is DJ Wayne with another observation of life. Join me tomorrow and help me write a novel! Yes I am asking for contributions for my next project and it is so easy.

FRIDAY 21ST SEPTEMBER 2012

In Yesterdays blog DJ Wayne gave a personal observation of life in general and asked the question why people are generaly not afraid to talk to other people, who they have never ever met, whilst out walking across the hills and trails. Today I am asking for volunteers to assist me in writing my next novel! You do not have to be a literary expert or even a master of the common tongue, all you need is to put a word, sentence or paragrapgh together and use your imagination.

As you are aware DJ Wayne is the famous author of two books "Not so perfect cooking", and "Chooooon a pictorial history of seaforsurf radio", and I would like you all to be part of our next project. In your personal copy of "Not so perfect cooking", if you do not have one it is available for purchase via Amazon at a very reasonable price, there are stories from the ABC game (copyright DJ Wayne) and this is what we will be using to write our novel.

This is going to be so good and I would like as many people to join in as possible. All you have to do is remember the next letter of the British alphabet (I do know Greek but it will not really work out!) Then you think of how you will like the story to progress, and from that point it is a personal view. It could follow the story line or fly of at a tangent into the netherworld of time and space. It could be futuristic or maybe involve those trolls and other creatures from the underworld. Don't forget the lovely fairies and Queens of lands forgotten. Oh and also the beautiful unicorns.

Get it?, if not, consult your personal copy of NSPC! I will start us off!

A gentlemen called Rodney was thinking about life in general and what he could do to enhance his way of life. Afterall he was quite wealthy and did not want for anything.

His house, which he rented, was not perfect ,but it kept out the rain and wind. In fact it was very much upmarket from the corrigated shed that DJ Wayne and Mrs DJ Wayne live in the Fens. Rodney was also owner of a mare with the name of Sheila. A lovely mare, which assisted in the day to day transportation of goods to and from the local market. Rodney was not married but always dreamed of meeting a local girl and raising afamily and this was foremost in his mind most days. There was something missing in his life and it needed to be filled before he became too old, after all he was getting on a little now, twenty five getting on for twenty six, time may be running out.

Today, he thought to himself, today will be different, there is a warm breeze and the sun is shinning across the fens. That allways makes a difference especially when the farmers have stopped harvesting and the mice and spiders have found new homes. As he harnessed Sheila, who had her nose in a feed bag, he whistled to himself and was in such a jolly mood he skipped and jogged to his made up tune. I could be a DJ on the radio, he thought to himself, I have rhythm and those blues.

So off they went down the dusty track, but before he had travelled a hundred yards he abruptly stopped, because there in the middle of the road was a...

Your turn, it starts with **B**, off you go. The story continues..

Update: It is absolutely amazing how the human mind works! I was on air and asked our SSR listeners to join me in the ABC game after I had started the story off with the letter A. The response was far more than I had hoped for. The continuing story ranged from a single word to, in some cases, over a page. The ABC project will continue and I thank all the contributors who put pen to paper although in most cases, if not all, fingers to keyboards. I hope to publish the finished story very soon. You may still contribute a "letter" by emailing your verse to wayne@whittleseasurf.com

SATURDAY 22ND SEPTEMBER 2012

As I have said many times, it is a funny old world. We have heard Nick Clegg saying "sorry", for promising at the 2010 election not to increase tuition fees. He said "We made a pledge, we did not stick to it, and for that I am sorry." The eventual decision by the coalition was to lift the cap on fees to £9,000. Was the "sorry" video edited by Frogbeat?

The government chief whip, Andrew Mitchell, got into hot water this week. Allegedly he called the police "f**king plebs" when they refused to open the street's gates for him. He has apologised and denied he actually used certain words but who would you believe a member of the cabinet or a police officer in the security service, who puts his life on the line every day? I know where I would put my money. Seems to me the police are in the firing line from the government as well as the thugs, murderers and rogues. Oh, and Ken Clarke has defended Andrew Mitchell calling him a "perfectly reasonable man". We are also very safe in our houses! There has been a spate of electrical fires so the Mayor of London has told the London Fire and Emergency Planning Authority it needs to save £65 million over the next two years. It has produced various plans, one of which would see a quarter of the capital's fire stations closing and 800 fire-fighters losing their jobs. You wait until the first disaster happens above or below ground, cabinet ministers will be running like scolded rabbits for cover and denying they had anything to do with it. Makes you feel great doesn't it?

Update 1: Friday 12th October 2012 Andrew Mitchell still denies he called the police security at the gates "plebs", so that must mean the police are liars! He has a meeting arranged with representatives of the police today so oh to be a fly on the wall, not just to listen but to see him squirm!

Update 2: Mr Mitchell resigned on Friday 19th October 2012, more than five weeks after a confrontation with Downing Street police officers, saying his position had become untenable. Tory peer Lord Tebbit said Mr Cameron had allowed "this dog of a coalition government" to look incompetent. Mr Mitchell has admitted swearing during the confrontation, over whether he could take his bicycle through the main gate in Downing Street, but denies claims he called the officers "plebs". We will see!!

Update 3: This story is going to run and run. Apparently there are now witnesses to "plebgate", with one being an off duty policeman.

SUNDAY 23RD SEPTEMBER 2012

There are some things that are a blatant infringement of an individual's personal rights and I am sure you could name a few yourselves, and I would put money on the nose that some are technology related. The one that is cracking my gears is automated telephone calls picking your number at random. For instance, the PPI help line, and the Accident compensation helpline. We are being plagued by them.

"We have it on record you can claim compensation for a recent accident", no you do not, I have not had one! "We have it on record you are entitles to up to £4000 compensation for a miss sold PPI", no you do not, I have never have never taken out a PPI in my life!

Ring ring

"Hello" I say.

"Hello sir how are you today?" You just know it is going to be an irritating call by the "how are you today?"

"not sure yet!" I respond.

"OK, have you had an accident in the last five years?" the caller enquires.

"You tell me, after all you called me" I reply.

"Have you had an accident in the last five years?" the caller asks again?

This goes on for a little while until I realise it is my tea break and I really do need to go.

"What is your name", I ask

"My name", he says puzzled, "Yes your name", I ask yet again

"It is Abu", ah at last we are getting somewhere.

"Right then Abu, if you do not stop ringing me and enquiring how I am today and asking other irrelevant questions I am going to report you to the Ombudsman for harassment and not only that I will find you and stick your telephone handset where the sun does not shine, understand Abu?"

"Yes Sir, thank you, have a nice day"

MONDAY 24TH SEPTEMBER 2012

I do not really understand the UK vehicle road tax system. It seems to be so outdated and not fit for purpose. After all the tax collected allegedly goes towards the upkeep and maintenance of the public highway. Now you and I know very well that is not the case as all revenue collected in various taxes goes into one big bottomless pit to be divided out willy nilly on the whim of a cabinet minister. Yes we do have a tax tier system but as I understand it the larger and older the car the more money is required to tax the vehicle. How stupid is that. I have a 4x4 because I want one, it is far from new as they are expensive to purchase. The tax for the year is nearly £300 but I drive less than 1000 miles a year as I only use it to transport my two dogs to the kennels and back when we go on holiday. That is not wearing out the roads! I propose a far fairer system which takes in to account how your vehicle would wear out the public highways dependent on the number of miles travelled. All this can be confirmed each year when the vehicle goes in to the garage for the annual MOT.

0-1000 miles £50 per annum

1001 – 10,000 miles £100 per annum

10,001 – 20,000 miles £200 per annum

20,001 – 50,000 miles £250 per annum

Over 50000 miles £400 per annum

This is a much fairer system and will be in DJ Wayne's election manifesto!

TUESDAY 25TH SEPTEMBER 2012

I am still being plagued by text messages from PPI and Accident help lines who are offering me serious amounts of cash if I make a claim. Now, I have been through this time and time again at home via text messages and even at work. I am of course tempted to make a claim however I do not really think I qualify although the people on the other end of the telephone tell me I definitely am eligible. One piece of good news however, I did ask the question again, "how did your organization get my telephone number?" At which point the telephone receiver is usually slammed down! Today a very helpful operator informed me to have your telephone number removed from the database email eazydigitalmarketing@gmail.com and it will be done. I do not have a lot of faith in these institutions keeping their word but it is certainly worth a try and I urge you all to do it if it stops these texts and calls invading your privacy.

Update 1: Make a note of eazydigitalmarketing@gmail.com

WEDNESDAY 26TH SEPTEMBER 2012

Great news today Seafordsurf Radio in partnership with Marcel P and the Deltaphonics http://marcelpleasance.com/ are giving away a total of six CDs by the band in a great competition to mark the debut of their six track CD "Concrete". The CD tracks were mixed at laffingboymusic studios http://www.laffingboymusic.com/ in Peterborough and have been played exclusively on Seafordsurf Radio. The Board members and staff thank David the Manager of Marcel and the Deltaphonics for the opportunity to assist in promoting this fantastic new band. Tune in to www.seafordsurfradio.com week commencing 8th October for an opportunity in winning one of these exclusive CDs.

THURSDAY 27TH SEPTEMBER 2012

Interesting to read in the news today, fewer than six out of 10 pupils, 58%, passed the controversial new national phonics reading test in England, official statistics show. The test checks six-year-olds' ability to read aloud a mixture of 40 real and made-up words, sounding them out using the phonics system. There are a number of issues here. Why on earth can only 58% pass the so called test, but even more worrying why are they trying to read made up words? It beggars belief that the educational system has fallen so low that we as a Nation are unable to provide our children with the basic ability to read and possibly write as well. We have a long established English language with spellings of all words that cannot be changed! That is the law! According to The Oxford English Dictionary there are 171,476 words in current use, and 47,156 obsolete words. To this may be added around 9,500 derivative words included as subentries. There are of course new words being added every year which I suppose we could be forgiven if they are new and we incorrectly spell them. The point is, stop faffing about with the education system and teach our children correctly without using methods which do not actually teach them how to read and write. Education Minister? Oh that will be Leighton Andrews. Who?

FRIDAY 28TH SEPTEMBER 2012

Have you noticed that some supermarkets and other small retail outlets seem reluctant to give out itemised receipts at the till? This has happened to me on numerous occasions especially at the local small supermarket which starts with an N and ends with an A and it sounds like it is NICE. Now the point is when you are in a bit of a hurry and wish to purchase half a dozen items then it is a quick dash in, make the purchase and dash out again so stuff your change and receipt in your pocket and file it in the bin when you get home.

But how do you know if you have been charged the correct amount? How do you know if you have been overcharged? Now I believe there are two reasons why itemised till receipts are not handed out. Firstly, the amount of money saved, by halving the paper used at the tills. Secondly, you have no proof you may have been overcharged. My advice is always ask for your itemised receipt and check the details otherwise you could be ripped off.

SATURDAY 29TH SEPTEMBER 2012

What another great day it has been today. Up early catch the train to London Kings Cross and geocaching on Clapham Common, in the pub for a drink, something to eat and then the train home. Bang on! Well what actually happened was up late, catch the slow train to London Kings Cross, window shopping on Oxford Street, walk around the twelve floors of John Lewis, pub was closed down and we were starving, and to top it all we had to eat the excuses for chips that are sold in a fast food outlet that sounds Scottish! I digress, my rant today and I do feel a little guilty about it is about a Big Issue seller who was on his pitch outside the John Lewis flagship store in London. As we were passing we heard, "Big issue, Big issue", which of course can be heard in most Towns and Cities across Britain. "Will someone, anyone buy a big Issue today? He said. "Bloody Anybody?"

Now I have to say I have bought The Big Issue in the past and I do believe in the principle so I stopped retrieved a £1 I had secreted on my person and offered it to The Big Issue vendor. Apparently it was not enough, as there had been a price increase. The correct price was £2.50. That must be what they call "London prices". Anyway I found some loose change and made the vendor a happy chappy, and I feel like a born again Christian. Oh Lordy!

SUNDAY 30TH SEPTEMBER 2012

The previous day we had a day out in the metropolis of London which is always an exciting excursion and full of expectations and surprises. Our travel took us from Kings Cross, Clapham Common, Hyde Park and then to Wandsworth. Our journey involved the overland train, tube and bus.

Now, in the heart of London you would expect a diversity of visitors, cultures and languages but on the bus to Wandsworth it felt like I was the visitor. There must have been seventy people on that bus and I was the one speaking a foreign language! I thought I was joining the throngs travelling to immigration control! I got told off as well!

The bell rang to indicate a passenger alighting the bus and one person said "jabber jabber jabber", which threw me for a while until she looked me in the eye and said again, "jabber jabber jabber". Oh dear what have I done now? Her arms began to wave faster than a wind turbine on the Fens but not so rhythmically. "Jabber bus jabber off jabber jabber chair jabber here jabber", dirty look!

Ah, it became clear I was standing blocking the wheelchair access and the individual was trying to manoeuvre to turn the chair on a euro to depart from the bus. I moved to the left, I moved to the right and then back to the left, space was at a premium.

"Jabber move jabber",

I did a pirouette that any accomplished ballet instructor would have been proud of and moved swiftly out of the vicinity. Well done me. "jabber ", "No jabber problem" I said, "it was a jabber pleasure", as the wheelchair ran over my toe! I was well and truly jabbered!

MONDAY 1ST OCTOBER 2012

£3.5 million to build up your mussels! I read, with interest, an article, relating to the freshwater pearl mussel which is apparently an endangered species. Half of Europe's freshwater pearl mussels live in Britain, coincidence really as do half the European inhabitants! Anyway the endangered species is close to extinction due to pollution and widespread poaching. Seventy five per cent of the breeding sites have been damaged due to crooks steeling pearls. It is a sad story really and I do feel for the mussels. As the story goes a winkle walked in to a bar and pulled a muscle; but it was not a happy ending. I am sure there should be safeguards and more security around the sites but does it really warrant awarding £3.5 million to campaigners? We could save the money and give it to individuals who are cheating the benefit system or speed up immigration control so undesirables do not have to wait in long queues at passport control. Or, and this may be a little more radical, award some of it to the Big Issue seller who I met in London!

TUESDAY 2ND OCTOBER 2012

DNDIY - Jeremy Clarkson is the original Marmite man, you either love or hate him! But he does talk a lot of sense. Put to one side the comment about shooting all the strikers who cause such pain and difficulties for the ordinary person who just wish to get on a train or bus and be able to go to work. He asks the interesting questions. If you had a brain tumour would you conduct the operation yourself? If you fell down and broke a leg would you drive yourself in a make shift ambulance to the hospital and conduct the proceedings yourself. The answer is a resounding no.

Then why is it that when there is some electrical work that needs undertaking or plumbing that needs repairing that we believe we are capable of doing it? It takes years of learning and apprenticeships to understand about the technicalities of electricity and water. And yet a browse around the local D.I.Y store for a plug, socket, 3 core cable or pipe fittings and connectors and we believe we are skilled enough to undertake the task in hand. This is pure and utter folly and may be the reason why the casualty departments deal with many burns, scolds, broken limbs, eye damage and broken toes. There is also the issue that hundreds if not thousands of skilled tradesmen who are laid off because the average person believes they can do the job without any knowledge and experience. D.I.Y does not work, get the experts in. D.N.D.I.Y – Do Not Do It Yourself. You know it makes sense and it may save your life!

WEDNESDAY 3RD OCTOBER 2012

There's a guy works down the chip shop swears he's Elvis was a hit in 1981 by singer Kirsty MacColl. Unfortunately she passed away in a freak accident in the year 2000 but that song with some strange lyrics stays with us. Why do I mention it in my blog do you ask? Well, coincidently The King's daughter Lisa Marie actually works in a chippy. Lisa regularly helps out in a mobile chippy wrapping customers cod and chips. Why? Apparently, according to the owners "she likes to see how we live". Lisa resides in her £9million home and rumour has it that we are all invited round to "see how she lives". Not sure about it myself can't stand the smell of old fish, rancid oil and old takeaway wrappers. Each to their own, I suppose.

THURSDAY 4TH OCTOBER 2012

Here we go yet again, and is this any surprise to any of us? Headline in the newspaper today: Overseas "health tourists" costing NHS at least £40 million" Hospitals in England and Wales are obliged to ensure NHS patients have lived in the UK for the past twelve months but Health Minister Anna Soubry admitted the system for identifying people who are not entitled to free care is "complex and at time flawed." Let's just mull over that for a minute. When I had a hospital appointment to see a Consultant I was advised by letter which stated the criteria for free treatment. Any two of the following: Utility bill in your name, Council Tax invoice also in your name, passport, driving licence, and social security documents etc etc. These documents give some sort of indication who is trying to get the treatment, so what is so complex about that?
Oh, and by the way on that and subsequent visits I never got asked to show those documents. That is the bit which is flawed. Hospitals are in a mess, bogged down with internal red tape, statistics and league tables ordered by the bureaucrats who are supposed to be running them, it is not surprising the basic rules and regulations are not adhered to. £40 million mmmmm what could we do with £40 million......

FRIDAY 5TH OCTOBER 2012

Sad news today as reported in the BBC, although it may not come as a surprise to some of us! Apparently and it is official. France is a dump! Now the French have been saying the UK is a land of fat ignorant peasants since the year dot, so what has changed? France has an unemployment rate of three million. Growth is zero and the Eurostar terminal at Gare du Nord is full of beggars, thieves and organised gangs who would whip your trousers off to get at your crown jewels before you could say oo la la where are my onions and garlic!

There is no comparison with the GB feel good factor and high public spirits. For once we can shout from the hill tops "It is great to be British". But there are still comparisons to be made. Taxes are rising and manufacturing closing down. There is gang warfare with knife and gun crime. The national handball team recently won the Olympics but this week several stars of the side have been arrested for match fixing. He who laughs last laughs the loudest. Still think Blackpool Tower is better than the Eiffel Tower and we have had a bumper year of slugs and snails, so crepe suzette and a bois noueux, hache affilee! Bon appétit

SATURDAY 6TH OCTOBER 2012

Who would walk naked from Land's End to John O'Groats, twice? Who has been arrested more times for nudity than MPs have had to apologise and say sorry? Who has spent over six years in prison, some in solitary confinement, for being naked in public? Mr Steven Brocklehurst, that's who! Mr Brocklehurst, better known as the naked rambler, is campaigning for the right to be naked in public at all times. He is of course fighting for all of us, or is he? I am not too sure if I would wish to walk about naked all day, after all it gets pretty nippy around the nether region on these autumnal nights. Would you wish to do your shopping in Tesco's and take a slow walk around the chillers and freezers searching for your frozen fish and ice lollies. I don't think so! Anyway, the Courts are losing patience with the naked rambler but on one occasion the former marine was allowed to walk away from Perth prison without wearing clothes. Not sure of the reasoning behind that one as that was the reason he was incarcerated in the first place. Chief Superintendent Andy McCann said, "We asked him to show a bit of consideration and only arrest him if his behaviour was gratuitous". However he must have shown off to much of his bits and he was back in court within three days. It costs a minimum of £40,000 a year to keep a prisoner in Scotland so at the moment without adding court fees it has cost near a quarter of a million Scottish squids. There has just got to be a better way of dealing with this. Answers on a postcard or email wayne@whittleseasurf.com

SUNDAY 7TH OCTOBER 2012

Now as you know, I am not one to complain! Well maybe a little. I get up early in the morning, not just to take the dogs out for their morning walk but also to miss the traffic in the morning rush hour, you know, the one which starts from seven in the morning until noon, and then the evening rush hour commences noon until 7 pm. Why do we call it the rush hour? Anyway this morning, I think, I encountered more than my fair share of obstructions. It commenced even before I had left the village with not one but two slow moving tractors and I do not mean a tiny Massy Ferguson I mean a huge MF (Massey Ferguson). However I am not one to complain about the agricultural farmers getting up early to plough as they need to get it completed before the weather changes.

No, it is the refuse collectors who are parked up with all lights blazing and not a lot going on. It is the very slow moving road sweeper, why do they have to clean the roads in the rush hour anyway? It is the brigade of small grass cutter vehicles which seem to appear out of thin air and surround you just to make sure you do not take a detour. Ah the joys of driving!

MONDAY 8TH OCTOBER 2012

We have had the joys of the Liberal Democrats party conference and the funny faces at the Labour party conference and now it is the turn of the conservatives. The smiles, promises and the feel good factor, it is so good to know we are in safe secure hands that sweep us up to their bosoms and promise to take us to Valhalla, the majestic, enormous hall located in Asgard, ruled over by the god Odin. Although to be fair it is usually the dead who travel to Valhalla, and they are the selected fifty percent. A little like the conservative promises really. "New" proposals to cut the social benefit to over fifty percent of recipients will be dead in the water. "New" Proposals to tax the very rich will be dead in the water. Nothing yet about the extortionate rate of tax on fuel! Nothing yet about a reduction of VAT which is only so high, because we give most of it away to assist the failing economies of Europe? Oh, one piece of good news is that George Osborne confirmed on radio five live that the average take home pay is £500 per week, and I thought I was Mr. Average!!! I wish.

TUESDAY 9TH OCTOBER 2012

A strange phenomenon has hit the London underground system, and now that it has been reported in the national press no doubt it will increase. If you are a regular commuter then you will know how to behave and adhere to the unwritten etiquette of the traveller. But how much attention do you actually pay? The etiquette states that you sit in your seat, if you manage to get one, and have the following options to choose from. 1. Pretend to read your newspaper, 2. Read a novel. 3. Read your kindle and look smug. 4. Play aimlessly with your mobile phone, or 5. Listen to music on your mobile phone but you need to keep your eyes shut and have the music turned up so loud as to annoy your fellow passengers within a hundred yard radius! If you are brave enough start having a glance around you but be sure to avoid eye contact at all costs as this will lead to fellow passengers having to look away quickly! The adverts and signage have all become familiar as is the underground map which is located on the carriage walls. It is all clutter of course so you would be excused for not noticing any subtle changes. Take the following examples which have been spotted: "No eye contact penalty £200." "We apologise for any incontinence caused during these engineering works." "Peak hours may necessitate you let other people sit on your lap." These are a few of a growing number of guerrilla stickers that have recently appeared on the network. They use the same fonts and designs as London Underground's famous branding. Graffiti or street art? The choice is yours!

WEDNESDAY 10TH OCTOBER 2012

The Conservative Party conference has been and gone for 2012, and you may have to be excused for not tuning in, listening and digesting every word. I for one would go to Afghanistan or Pakistan if I wanted to listen to a Drone! That is not to say I did not enjoy a few of the snippets of interesting facts which materialised in between the promises and apologies. There was a small debate over taxes although nothing exciting happened on that front. The focus was on reforming the system and making the rich pay more, yippee, that will drive the Business Magnates overseas then along with the entrepreneurs who may have created new jobs! By the way the current tax system can be easily understood by everyone and there is no excuse for not knowing it, after all it is only 12,000 pages long. Easy peasy! Oh by the way we spend more on social benefits than we do on the Police force!

THURSDAY 11TH OCTOBER 2012

As you may gather from these blogs scroungers, benefit cheats and children with bad manners really get my back up. Scroungers and benefit cheats are stealing not just my money but yours as well, so let's see some action from the government and put an end to it. Remember there are two further countries joining the EU in 2014, Bulgaria and Romania, so the floodgates will rise and there will be an influx of people coming into Britain to claim their benefits, housing, free NHS treatment without returning anything to the state. Remember these people descend from gypsies so their way of living is to beg steal and borrow. Do something about it now before the British way of living will be nothing more than a third world country. Speakers corner in Hyde Park London. An ideal location for DJ Wayne

FRIDAY 12TH OCTOBER 2012

How are you coping with your telephone bill? After all you just have to look at the telephone and another fifty pence is added to the bill! But could you cope with this? A woman in south-west France has received a demand for nearly 12 quadrillion Euros, which is quite a large amount in anybody's language. Solenne San Jose, from Pessac outside Bordeaux, said she received a huge shock when she opened the bill for 11,721,000,000,000,000 Euros (£9.4qn), which is nearly 6,000 times France's annual economic output. She said she nearly had a heart attack when she opened the envelope and saw all the zeros! She knew it was a lot but could not work out how much it actually was. The phone company, Bouygues Telecom, initially told her there was nothing they could do to amend the computer-generated statement and later offered to set up instalments to pay off the bill. What? In the end, the company admitted the bill should have been for 117.21 Euros only and eventually waived it altogether. How very kind! It has also apologised for the error which it says was down to a printing error and a subsequent misunderstanding between the client and staff at their call centre. Printing error, I think it was more than a printing error, and why is it there is always a misunderstanding" between client and staff when a call centre is involved? As a good will gesture the telephone company waived the real amount she owed. Ah how kind. One good thing though, at least we know telephone companies and call centres are just inept and prone to errors in other countries besides the UK!

SATURDAY 13TH OCTOBER 2012

SSR Daily

Wednesday, December 28, 2011

DJ Wayne teases audience

Yet again the Seafordsurf Radio switchboard was jammed again during the first half hour of the Whittlesey Scene And Heard Show. Many listeners had tuned in to play the infamous, 'How Much To Rent' which had been widely promoted throughout the day. At 29 minutes past eight Wayne let rip his jingle to an excited audience who had been whipped to a near frenzy with the anticipation of the rent boys/girls game going ahead, only to announce that would all be coming up later. One resident, a greenskeeper at nearby Orton Meadows Golf Course, was furious and ranted,'Why does he do this to us, we were waiting to see a soap on the TV, my Irene was disappointed, she insisted on staying for the quiz but annoyed about missing the soap.' DJ Wayne later said, 'Don't blame me, blame the board.'

SUNDAY 14TH OCTOBER 2012

Are we as strong and hardy as our ancestors? This has always been debatable. After all with social welfare and our luxurious living, compared to years ago, we may not be as fit as our forebears. Well today it is official, we are a bunch of wimps who run for shelter at the first sight of, and yes you have guessed it, rain! Yes, that nasty stuff that falls out of the sky and belts you around the head and soaks you to the skin. My how terrifying it is. The Battle of Hastings was fought on 14 October 1066 and saw the victory of William, Duke of Normandy who defeated the English army led by King Harold II. Boo to the Frenchies. The battle was just as exciting as being poked in the eye with a sharp stick. Normally there is a two day re-enactment which takes place near Battle Abbey, East Sussex on the anniversary, and this year it marks 946 years, but it has been cancelled due to rain. King Harold must be turning in his grave! Why do we celebrate the battle, after all the English lost to the French and

William ascended the throne? One very good reason; it marked the last successful foreign invasion of the British Isles. Let's keep it that way and shut down the borders, NOW!

MONDAY 15TH OCTOBER 2012

Well, here is a coincidence, another Army story. If Phillip Hammond gets his way the Territorial Army (TA) will be renamed, and this is an idea that just popped into his head, "The Army Reserve". He must have thought about that when he was sitting on the toilet reading his copy of Private Eye, as I am sure he must have been featured in there somewhere. Why reorganise and rebrand the TA. It will cost millions in consultancy and advisors fees. Britain has had a reserve of part-time or retired soldiers - often known as yeomanary - since the Middle Ages. It was mobilised just before World War I and its soldiers fought alongside regular soldiers in the trenches of northern France. In 1920 it became the Territorial Army and in 1939 it was doubled in size as war clouds approached again. As part of the recent defence review, the numbers of regular soldiers is set to fall from 102,000 to 82,000, while reservists will double to 30,000. Now I am not a skilled mathematician or an accountant but even I know it will cost more to run the two Armies if those figures are to be believed. And for what? Mr Hammond has said he hoped that a number of those leaving the slimmed down regular forces would join the reserves and "help change the ethos". Oh I am sure they will all volunteer to do that after they have just been sacked! No Mr Hammond. Leave the TA alone to support the brave soldiers fighting in foreign lands where they should not be anyway. If you wish to save millions of pounds then do not send the British Army to got forsaken countries to save poor souls who would shoot you in the back for a price of a liquorish stick.

TUESDAY 16TH OCTOBER 2012

Let's hope there will be no uprisings, Arab springs, or internal strife in these "stans!" The West has a habit of getting involved and "helping out", to the detrimental effect to the tax payers in the UK. There is also the issue with social security payments and housing for all the "refugees" who flee the oppression of their own lands only to try and convert the West in to some strange fanatical belief. How strange when people are free it is never good enough! So this is the list of "Stans" to assist you in practicing the pronunciation:-

Afghanistan, Kazakhstan, Kyrgyzstan, Pakistan, Tajikistan, Turkmenistan,Uzbekistan, Hayastan, Bashk ortostan, Tatarstan, Dagestan, Stanley Kubrick, Karakalpakstan, Uzbekistan, Balochistan, Pakistan, Gilgit–Baltistan, Gobustan,
Rayon, Azerbaijan, Golestan, Khuzestan ,Lorestan, Nurestan, Rajasthan,Sistan ,
Baluchestan, Balochistan, Baltistan, Bantustan, Cholistan, Dardistan,Dashtestan, Hazarastan, Stan Laurel, Hindustan, Kafiristan, Stanstead Airport, Nuristan Stanley
Gibbons, Kohistan, Kurdistan, Larestan, Stan Boardman,Lezgistan, Dagestan,
Azerbaijan, Mehrestan, Sistan, Baluchestan,Moghulistan, Mughalistan, Kazakhstan,
Kyrgyzstan, North Waziristan,Pashtunistan, Registan, Russian Turkestan , Sakastan, Saraikistan,
Stanley Livingston, Sistan, South Waziristan, Tabaristan, Talyshistan, Tangestan,Tocharistan,
Tukharistan, Tokharistan, Turkestan, Turkistan, Uyghurstan,Zabulistan,

WEDNESDAY 17TH OCTOBER 2012

I really do not understand the euphoria over the ruling not to extradite the British hacker Gary McKinnon. McKinnon has been accused of hacking into more than 90 unclassified Pentagon and NASA systems in 2001 and 2002, causing some of them to crash. Authorities say his actions led to

$900,000 in damages. McKinnon, who was dubbed the "biggest military computer hack of all time" by U.S. authorities, has admitted to accessing U.S. government computers more than a decade ago, but claims he did so only to find proof of a military cover up regarding the existence of UFO's. McKinnon allegedly left a message on one Army computer he breached in 2002, saying, "U.S. foreign policy is akin to government-sponsored terrorism these days. Forgive me for being blunt but he is a member of the scumbag society! It is scum hackers like him who scam millions from personal bank accounts and cause misery to thousands of honest people. It is scumbags like him who do not think twice over the misery they cause to ordinary people and have no regard to what happens to them. He is a member of the same clan who scam millions from individuals when they hack in to your personal computers, wipe out your bank account and leave a virus. It is pathetic that the likes of people in power have halted the extradition because he may commit suicide. That is no reason at all to stop the judicial process. It is pathetic that the likes of Peterborough MP Stewart Jackson, claims it a "victory". I say to you Mr. Jackson will you think the same when you have had your bank account hacked and all your funds distributed to some drugs baron in Mogadishu? Only one place for fraudsters, hackers and scumbags behind bars, without a computer, where they belong!

THURSDAY 18TH OCTOBER 2012

This could have an impact on your neighbours. Apparently you can choose and change the name of your wireless internet which is visible when you do a search near your location. Users have been setting their network names to send messages to their neighbours. Names like, "Terror network", "Virus Detected Shutting Down", "Pretty fly for a Wi-Fi "and "Wi Believe I Can Fi" have all been spotted. However that sounds rather innocent compared to these which may be having a dig at their neighbours: "Stop Stealing My Paper!" so the neighbour replies "FYI, I Don't Read It I Just Throw It Away!" "You're music is annoying!" is followed by "Your grammar is more annoying!" "Meat is Murder" alongside "Meat is delicious!!!" "Shut The Barking Dog Up No 7", "Stop slamming the door!!!", "Stop wearing heels!", "Shut up", "Stop running", "Stop shouting!", "Shut it Shoreditch" and "Stop using taps" , Particular types of noise complaints dominate. Chief among these is sex. Popular names are "We can hear you having sex" and 'StopHavingSoMuchSex'. Names also seen are, "getYourOwnInternet", "EatTheChildrenFirst". For the righteous and honest wifi users we have "Covet not thy neighbour's Wi-Fi" and "Thou shalt not steal!" Ah technology I love it! Honest!

FRIDAY 19TH OCTOBER 2012

Have you ever parked your vehicle in a car park, completed your shopping, and returned to the car park only to wake up to the stark realisation you are unable to remember where you left it. That leads to the walking up and down the level you thought you had left it and then, god forbid, searching other levels! I am sure most of us have been there. However, a German man has just been reunited with his car two years after forgetting where he parked it. When he failed to locate the vehicle the next morning, he reported it missing to police in Munich. The missing car was eventually discovered, by chance, after a traffic warden noticed its inspection sticker had expired. The elusive car was in a parking lot 2.5 miles away from where the craftsman thought he had parked and had searched two years earlier. Perhaps that is a lesson for all of us!

SATURDAY 20TH OCTOBER 2012

Unbeaten in 14 consecutive victories!

Career prize money of more than £3 million!
Owned by Arab Prince Khalid Abdullah!
Valued at £100m!
Retired and put out to stud!
Bedding over 150 females every year!
Now which Premier league football player would that be, I hear you ask? Or it could be a fat cat politician in Parliament. No, it is Frankel, maybe the greatest racing horse of all time. I just wish I had the foresight to back him in all fourteen races. Hey Ho!

SUNDAY 21ST OCTOBER 2012

It should not surprise me but I am astounded by the number of stupid idiots there are at football stadiums. There are elements of the crowds who are pathetic and should be locked up in a derelict zoo with the doors welded together. The other day there was the disgusting behaviour of the Serbian supporters who taunted certain players in the under twenty ones game. The latest episode involved a man running on to the pitch after Leeds had equalised in the game on Friday. Sheffield Wednesday's Chris Kirkland, required treatment after being struck in the face during the game against Leeds United. I could not believe my eyes as I was watching the game. A 21-year-old man has been arrested on suspicion of assault after a goalkeeper was attacked during a Championship football match. Gloucestershire Police said a man from Cheltenham had been arrested on suspicion of assault. He will go through the judicial system of course. You know, arrested, bailed, magistrates court, a fine and then make some money from his story. An alternative solution is arrest, not bailed, Crown court and a prison sentence. If he is claiming social benefits of any kind they should be stopped at once. The pathetic moron!

Update 1: The culprit, Aaron Cawley has been named and shamed. The twenty one year old has been jailed for 16 weeks and a five year football banning order. The court heard Cawley had been drinking heavily and had already breached two previous banning orders so I am not really convinced the punishment will work.

MONDAY 22ND OCTOBER 2012

I would like to say thank you to the inconsiderate member of the close who had a bonfire in their back garden yesterday afternoon. Not sure what they were burning, it could have been his underwear but the smoke was as thick as his brain cells! It was as thick as fog and we had to ensure the conservatory doors and all the windows were shut. Well, I just had to go and have a look, as I thought the house was on fire but no, it was a bonfire. I met the adjacent neighbour and she was also vocal about what was happening Not sure if anyone actually complained to the culprit but I am sure I will be receiving a letter from the Council as that is what happened last time a bonfire was lit in the close, and it was not in my garden! Community relations Ay!

TUESDAY 23RD OCTOBER 2012

Iain Duncan Smith, the current Works and Pensions secretary, should read DJ Wayne's blog a little more often and he may be aware of some of the feelings of ordinary people. He says there should not be a "something for nothing" culture, which is fair enough, so why are we giving free National Health care to anybody who enters this Country? There is more than enough evidence at hand that shows immigrants, legal and illegal are receiving the benefits without putting a penny into the pot.

We are mugs in this Country. Not sure about you but I pay enough Income Tax, NI, VAT and other stealth taxes to support a Nation, but obviously not this one. When is the government going to wake up and stop this rot?

WEDNESDAY 24TH OCTOBER 2012

Ian Duncan Smith is in the news again. He has hit on the bright idea of capping child-related benefits for families. Now far be it for me to put fuel on the fire but I have been saying this for years. Oh the "do-gooders" will throw their hands up in the air and scream that we will all live in poverty and our children will be paupers and have to go to work down the mines. Iain Duncan Smith argues that stopping the current system, where families get more benefits the more children they have, was among changes being considered. Does he not realize that has been happening for years and nobody has taken any notice of it? If two individuals arrive in this Country, they will be housed and register for free health care. Then ten children later with free housing benefit, council tax benefit, social security payments, child benefits for each of the offspring and other benefits they never need to work again. Well Duncan, put your money where your mouth is, and I do not mean another speech!

THURSDAY 25TH OCTOBER 2012

The town of Totnes in Devon prides itself, and quite rightly, over their stance not to have National chain shops in their area. They prefer the independent shops. Ah remember those days? That is when a Town did not look like a clone of the town a few miles away. The day when out of town "shopping centers" hit us saw the demise of the towns and indeed some cities as well. It was a national disaster and a disgrace. However in a strange turnaround South Hams District Council had approved plans by Costa Coffee to open in Fore Street, Totnes, but then Costa pulled out after it had "recognized the strength of feeling" against national brands in the town. At last common sense prevails and a great example of listening to the people.

FRIDAY 26TH OCTOBER 2012

In the news today Rowan Atkinson has launched a campaign demanding a change in the law that risks limiting free expression and feeds a 'creeping culture of censoriousness'. Mmmm fine words indeed, so what does it all mean to us all? Apparently, Section 5 of the 1986 Public Order Act which outlaws, "threatening, abusive or insulting words or behaviour that is likely to cause harassment, alarm or distress". That is on the statute books so basically there should not be any stand-up comics, TV comedy programs and certainly no magazines like Private eye and of course the Sun newspaper! Recent examples of the legislation being used have seen the arrest of a Christian preacher for telling a passer-by that homosexuality was sinful, a 16-year-old boy holding a placard that read "Scientology Is a Dangerous Cult", and a student who called a police horse 'gay'. A key part of the legislation is the use of the phrase "likely to cause", meaning that no-one actually has to be offended for an offence to have taken place. I say support Rowan Atkinson all the way otherwise you will offend someone and be arrested if you sneeze loudly, tell a joke or laugh at a saucy postcard!

SATURDAY 27TH OCTOBER 2012

As mentioned previously in this blog the NHS has got itself into a mess and no matter how much more public money is thrown in to the black hole it will not be able to heal the gaping wounds. In fact there is not a sticking plaster big enough to cover the gaping sore. Part of the problem, I believe is the constant chopping and changing of departments and responsibilities, none more so than the GP surgery itself. Yes, the old premises have been replaced by a new fit for purpose surgery but you just try getting an appointment. The odds are greater than winning the national lottery! The receptionist has absolute power over you, and woe betide if you get on the wrong side of them you would never be able to get to see a Doctor ever again. If your surgery offers "advance bookings", obviously for those with powers that can see into the future, then get in there quick. I, for one, have secured an appointment for one week's time just in case I am ill. After all yesterday I banged my head on the loft trapdoor, so I could have done with that appointment today, but there is little chance of getting one. If I remember I will bang my head again on the night prior to the appointment!

SUNDAY 28TH OCTOBER 2012

Have you visited your Post Office recently? No, I don't mean the local one (that has probably been closed down and boarded up in the guise of reducing costs!) I mean the main City Post Office. The one where you have to take a ticket, sit down, if there is a seat, and await your turn to be served. The thing is you will most likely have about twenty people in front of you no matter what time of day you attend. As well as the queue you will have to cope with other individual's body odour, bad breath, alcohol fumes, sneezing germs, coughing, spitting, snorting, bad language, moaning, groaning, loud rollicking laughter over bad jokes, babies in soiled nappies, ignorant people who try to push in saying they have lost their ticket and unruly children who are bored and end up trying to ransack the place. Then, when your number is called out and you rush to the desk you see a grumpy bad tempered member of staff who does not really want to be there and has no interest in serving you or answering your questions. Whatever happened to Customer Service?

MONDAY 29TH OCTOBER 2012

Talk about supermarket challenge and the trolley push, it is a challenge to get around the supermarket without having your toes and legs broken. I have spent hours analyzing this and come up with two categories of shoppers. Shopper number one is the mad dasher who needs to get round and complete their shopping in 5 nanoseconds. There are no obstacles in the way for this shopper. They barge, moan and push anyone who dares to get in their way. Shopper number two is a different kettle of fish. They meander their way through the aisles not really looking for anything in particular. The labels of the products need to be read and each loaf of bread has to be felt, squeezed and prodded before the decision is made not to have it. They must have their trolleys across the aisles so nobody can pass them by. If anybody dares to touch their personal trolley then woe betides the daggers and grumpy looks. No, it is the local shop for me!

TUESDAY 30TH OCTOBER 2012

In the news today, nearly one million households will be receiving letters from the UK tax authority this week about losing child benefit. Disgraceful! Families need the extra revenue to feed their hungry offspring. But wait minute, households where at least one person earns more than £50,000 will have the benefit reduced or stopped. Let me pass that one across you again. Households with at least one person earning more than £50K will be affected. So are you telling me these are the nation's poor and destitute? Are you telling me that people with an income of £50K and more are living on the breadline? NO I think not, and if they are then pass a wad of £50K to me please and I will try very hard to spend it. Part of the money that is paid out in Child benefits is what ordinary workers' pay in from their taxes. So you and I are giving our money to these "poor" families! Well that makes me feel even better then. Deputy Prime Minister Nick Clegg described the coalition's plan as an "excruciatingly difficult decision". Well not for me it is not. What he should be doing is stopping ALL subsidies and benefits to any family in this income bracket. Come on Government get a grip and only pay out to those who really need it!

WEDNESDAY 31ST OCTOBER 2012

Apparently new European tyre labelling could save money and lives. The laws which come into effect on 1 November 2012 should make it easier for consumers to make "educated choices" when purchase their tyres. Personally when I have needed to replace worn or damaged tyres I have always gone for a quality brand as recommended by the garage, after all they are the experts, aren't they? That could be the flaw in my argument of course. Do they recommend the correct tyre which is best for the vehicle and of course my pocket? I think perhaps not. So with new laws and new labelling I will have no problem choosing the tyre I need! One suggestion from me! Make it a law that these tyres are only fitted on vehicles which are fully taxed, insured and a valid MOT. That way it would really save lives and takes off the roads vehicles which are dangerous and should be scrapped. Just a thought!

THURSDAY 1ST NOVEMBER 2012

Can anybody tell me why the UK is giving India billions of pounds each year, in aide? It has been reported in the press India is racing up the league of rich nations. In fact its soaring economy will outstrip the UKs by 2022. Oh do you think India will take pity on us and start giving us our billions back then! I think not. David Cameron has decided to give India £1.4 billion between now and 2015. The sum is almost 1 per cent of Britain's own £159 billion debts. But does India really need our funds, and, perhaps more pertinently, what's happening to it when it gets there? It has been proved that much of our money is frittered away or stolen. This is a country that has its own space programme. Once again it has been proved that we British are stupid and in live in the shadow of our colonial past. Let India, the country that wanted independence be independent have the balls to say, "Mr UK we do not need your money any more. We will stop being a corrupt government, cancel the space programme and feed our own children, who at the moment are dying of starvation which can be avoided. Oh, and I want my part of the contribution returned.

Update No.1: Hot news 9th November 2012: The UK Government must be and should be reading D J Wayne's blog. The financial "aid" given to India is to be phased out by 2015. Support worth about £200m ($319m) will be phased out between now and 2015 and the UK's focus will then shift to offering technical assistance.

FRIDAY 2ND NOVEMBER 2012

Working in an office environment can be very dangerous as working in a production factory. For instance, there are staircases to be negotiated, nasty paper clips to be dealt with and the ultimate hazard, paper cuts.

These are so painful and makes any office workers day a misery. There is one temporary solution to this of course, superglue! Yes superglue, especially the little 5gm with the brush. Just undo the twist top take the brush out and spread across the paper cut on your finger. It works a treat. One hint of course, let it dry completely before going to the toilet!!

SATURDAY 3RD NOVEMBER 2012

XH558 Does that mean anything to you? No, well the XH558 is the last remaining Vulcan bomber which has kept the flag flying and its days may be numbered. The Vulcan bombers were once the UK's most potent nuclear deterrent and were on standby for a role in the Cuban missile crisis. The "tin triangle", which is more than 50 years old, needs "challenging modifications" to both wings which the trust that owns it has decided, cannot be funded. The Leicestershire-based Vulcan "To The Sky" trust, which bought the aircraft in 2005, says escalating costs and limited engine life mean soon it will be confined to the runway for limited displays. Upkeep of XH558 has been funded through public donations but the trust has come to the conclusion that the generosity that has kept her flying cannot meet the challenges ahead. More than £2m is needed each year to cover general maintenance, fuel and insurance, with any repairs needing additional funding. This icon of the British airwaves must be saved from extinction. Easy answer Mr Cameron divert some of the £1.4 billion we are giving India, they will not miss it!

SUNDAY 4TH NOVEMBER 2012

Peterborough council has been up to mischief once again. They agreed to a public consultation of the closure of two elderly care homes and disregarded everyone's views apart from their own. It is a sham, a farce and makes a mockery of ever holding a public consultation. The cabinet think they know what is best for their community rather than listening to them. The council was in a stunned silence when councillors decision to close Greenwood House, in South Parade, West Town, by the end of November and Welland House, in Poplar Avenue, Dogsthorpe in March. The cabinet unanimously agreed to the recommendation without a show of hands, prompting anger from the public gallery and on Twitter. The councillors were heckled by members of the public in the gallery. Protestors had written 51 letters against closure and secured 6,000 signatures on petitions opposing the closure of the homes during a consultation on their future. The closure will mean 30 people will have to be re-homed while 130 staff face redundancy at a cost to the council of £2 million. Where is the logic and sense in that? The public must keep this at the forefront of their minds when the next local elections are due. Get rid of the fat cats who are only in the chamber to better their business opportunities and make money in the guise of being a public servant.

MONDAY 5TH NOVEMBER 2012

Today I have grave news to share with you. So grave that you may be shocked in to silence and even disbelieve what I am saying. So here goes, "The honey monster does not care about you". I know, I know, calm down and take a deep breath. The honey monster is the front man to the very popular breakfast cereal "Sugar Puffs", but I believe he is a stooge and will only react when told to do so. In fact it may be hard to believe but I now have doubts that he is real and may not even exist. Why do I believe this I hear you scream! Well, in early October I purchased a packet of Sugar Puffs only to find, when I opened them, that they were burnt. They were well below the quality you would expect from the honey monster. My disappointment was so severe I wrote a letter to the consumer services department at Honey Monster foods outlining the problem. I have yet to receive a reply back. This is disgraceful and thus my belief in the existence of the honey monster has waned. How can I sleep at night?

Update No.1 10/11/12: See Sunday 11th November 2013!

TUESDAY 6TH NOVEMBER 2012

Oh here we go again, is it the silly season starting early? Immigration is top of the agenda yet again. I really do not understand the futile and lame excuses we get from this government, and the opposition parties are no better. This is a very small island and we have legal limits on immigrants who wish to settle in this country. What is wrong with theirs? Could it be no social security, no free housing, no child benefit, and no welfare? Once the limit has been reached then shut the door!

Illegal immigration is simple, if you do not have the right to settle here then go back to where you came from. Why is the UK so wimpy and gullible to a pair of sad eyes, just try it on the French and see what response you get from them. Illegal means illegal means illegal, I suggest every sitting MP looks it up in a dictionary just to remind them of its meaning. What has happened that makes me put fingers to keyboard yet again on this subject? Well, the UK Border Agency's attempts to clear a massive backlog of cases could become an amnesty for immigrants with no right to be in the UK.

What! Well do something constructive about it then. If a child does not do their homework, you do not say "oh leave it then"; no you assist and put more resources in to the issue. If the MP in charge of the UK Border patrol is unable to do the job then he should go and appoint a person who can!

WEDNESDAY 7TH NOVEMBER 2012

UKBA case backlog

· Current asylum cases 25,500
· Asylum "controlled archive" 74,000
· Current immigration cases: 3,500
· Immigration "controlled archive": 21,000
· Migration Refusal Pool 174,057
· Former foreign prisoners: 3,954
· Untraced former foreign prisoners: 53
· Total: 302,064
· Staff dealing with the problem 149
· MP in charge 1 · MP with the balls to do the job 0 · People who are fed up with illegal immigration millions

THURSDAY 8TH NOVEMBER 2012

What a great day in November for Geocaching in Whitby North Yorkshire. The sun is shining and off for a lovely walk. Ah, the geese are having a wander about as well. Let me take a picture of our feathered friends. That is when it went wrong.

Apparently they are shy and take offense to tourists with cameras, and chased us down the road, and by golly can they move and they can be quite vocal as well. Think I now know "Naff off or I will bite your bum, or other parts" in geese language. Ah bless em!

FRIDAY 9TH NOVEMBER 2012

Even in Whitby the mindless morons commit acts of vandalism. Why? Well if I knew the answer to that I would be worth a bob or two. There could be many reasons ranging from boredom, aggressive behaviour or just being a prat! These idiots cost the country a fortune and sadness to the owners, be it private of council owned, someone has to pay for the damage. I can only hope and wish that whoever does this damage there is a guiding light that makes them suffer for what they have done. Unfortunately of course they will probably become Councillors, MPs or fat cat bankers!

SATURDAY 10TH NOVEMBER 2012

What a lovely place this is. If you want to be transported back in time pay a visit to Grosmont in North Yorkshire. It takes you back to the British Rail days and it is a running line. It is not just for rail enthusiasts, take my word it is for all to enjoy those days gone by when railways were for all, not just those with a hundred pound to go fifty miles down the road.

SUNDAY 11TH NOVEMBER 2012

*****Hot news*****Hot News*****Hot News*****Hot News*****Hot News*****
After sending my second letter to the Honey monster I have to report a result and perhaps a little embarrassment. One thing that really makes me rant is bad customer service, hence the follow up letter to the Honey monster, pointing out he did not have the decency to reply. I now report I have a reply and a token apology of a £6.50 p postal order. Thank you Honey monster!

MONDAY12TH NOVEMBER 2012

Sometimes but not many times, words fail me. In the news today a school has banned a pupil from growing a moustache for a charity campaign because it says it is not an "inclusive" activity. What? Being bad mannered, sloppy, aggressive and bad mouthing the teachers is an "inclusive" activity then? Gus Hooker, 13, from Dunstable, Bedfordshire, wanted to take part in Movember, where men grow facial hair to raise money for Prostate Cancer UK. The Priory Academy said it was "not an activity that many children would be able to join in with". The schoolboy said he thought he could have raised "a fair bit" of money. He wanted to take part in the campaign, because his grandfather recently beat cancer. "Because I can grow a moustache, I reckon that if I did it I could raise a fair bit," he said. "I just wanted to show off my moustache, everyone wanted me to go for it." A spokesperson for the school said it could only support fundraising activities that are "entirely inclusive". "Fundraising is an inclusive activity with all pupils having the opportunity to participate regardless of age or gender," a statement said. Oh do me a favour, it is not easy to get some children to participate in any activity, so why not support the ones who show a bit of intelligence and try something different especially for their chosen charity. As a compromise, the school has allowed the teenager to organise a charity dress down day on 30 November, in which students will be allowed to wear fake moustaches for a £1 donation.

TUESDAY 13TH NOVEMBER 2012

Perhaps certain members of the UK government and members of Councils across the land could take a leaf out of Jose Mujica's book. Who is Jose Mujica I hear you ask? Well Jose is the President of Uruguay and is the world's poorest president. He lives on a ramshackle farm and gives away most of his pay. The water comes from a well in a yard, which is overgrown with weeds. Only two police officers and Manuela, a three-legged dog, keep watch outside. President Mujica has shunned the luxurious house that the Uruguayan state provides for its leaders and opted to stay at his wife's farmhouse, off a dirt road outside the capital, Montevideo. The president and his wife work the land themselves, growing flowers. He has been quoted as saying "I can live well with what I have." His luxurious automobile is a 1987 VW Beetle. What more can anybody ask for? Well, a damn lot according to MPs and Politicians whom some have reportedly fiddled their expenses and tax returns to get that extra schilling out of the state, and that means out of your pocket! Good on you Jose!

WEDNESDAY 14TH NOVEMBER 2012

I make no apologies over reporting this news story. Whilst the UK is very slowly coming out of recession, petrol prices are hitting our pockets and austerity measures are kicking in it is good to know that Government Agencies are doing their bit to assist with the deficit. Oh hold on I have got that wrong, let me recap. Maritime officials have spent almost £20,000 sending four people to an annual boat show in Monaco. The Maritime and Coastguard Agency paid for the Monaco Yacht Show trip with one employee flying business class.

The Taxpayers' Alliance has quite rightly criticised the decision to spend money on "expensive trips to swanky destinations". Given that cuts are being made to the coastguard budget, spending so much money on a trip to Monaco will infuriate taxpayers. Is this the same coastguard who have made employees redundant and closed down some coastal stations? Oh yes, eight local coastguard stations across the UK have been cut as a result of a restructuring programme with a loss of 159 jobs. The co-ordination centres at Forth, Clyde, Great Yarmouth, Liverpool, Thames, Swansea, Brixham and Portland will all close by March 2015. This is a farce and should be dealt with. The management and decision makers are pathetic and should be removed if they are unable to conduct their business in a proper manner. If they need any advice then they know where I am!

THURSDAY 15 NOVEMBER 2012

It really does make you wonder what on earth is going on in this country. Is it a country of democracy and free speech? Not anymore it's not! A man, who is a Christian, had been demoted in his job, lost his managerial position and had a 40% salary cut writing on Face book "a gay wedding held in a church was equality too far." What is wrong about making a comment of this nature? At this rate all of the daily newspapers would be taken to court, the editors hung drawn and quartered for saying the honey monster does not care about his customers! Oops I had better watch my step on that one! Of course if you were a Muslim cleric and had a few rants nobody would be able to touch you for it anyway! This country has a proud record of fighting for free speech. Don't knock it. On the plus side Mr. Smith has won a breach of contract action against his employers after claiming they had acted unlawfully in demoting him. In a statement he said: "Something has poisoned the atmosphere in Britain, where an honest man like me can be punished for making perfectly polite remarks about the importance of marriage. I am with you on that one!

FRIDAY 16TH NOVEMBER 2012

Have I missed a very important event that has captured the imagination of people across the length and breadth of the UK? The vey talking point in all the pubs and leading to in depth discussions and verbal outbursts across the country? Maybe! I am not too sure? I am of course referring to the elections of the Police commissioners, and living in a democracy as we do, all eligible voters had the opportunity to vote for their candidate. That is of course if you were able to find out who they were and what they stood for! Bye elections are notorious for low turnout but now a polling station in Gwent has the record turnout of zero. If I had known I would have applied for the £70,000 salary and would have only needed one vote and I am sure I could have got that from a local sheep or the neighbourhood donkey or chicken! I have now missed the opportunity until the next occasion. The turnout across Gwent was 14.3%. A spoken said "It's just apathy. I think apathy rules when it comes to politics in general," he said. "People are more concerned with the bigger picture like the recession." He probably has a valid point on that one. If there was a vote to reduce the excessive tax on petrol or lower the extortionate amount we pay in road tax then I would be at the front of the queue!

SATURDAY 17TH NOVEMBER 2012

We all know there are not so very nice individuals within our community. We see them nearly every day exhibiting anti-social behaviour, aggressive and bad mannered, litter louts and so called travellers leaving disgusting mess wherever they go! However what is worse than all those? Scumbags who steal "poppy boxes," which have been filled with coins by a caring and grateful members of the community that is who! Up to ten boxes have been stolen within the Peterborough area alone. Police have CCTV of two people they want for questioning in connection with the thefts. One member of the public said "stealing charity boxes is a particular low act", another said, "It makes me feel absolutely sick inside". Personally I could think of other phrases which are far harsher that those! What do you think? Please comment email wayne@whittleseasurf.com

SUNDAY 18TH NOVEMBER 2012

Oscar Wilde's "A picture of Dorian Gray" 78,462 words
Erich Remarque's "All quiet on the western front" 61,922 words
DJ Wayne's Blog Priceless!

MONDAY 19TH NOVEMBER 2012

You have heard it here first on DJ Wayne's blog. Councillors can be, and have been, jack assess when it comes to making decisions which can affect us all. But this news story saddens me. A donkey with a passion for politics has been banned from running in Ecuador's local council elections after officials ruled it was an insult to the opposition. While the candidate may look like a bit of a jackass, he is hugely popular with voters, who have been campaigning to get him elected in the city of Guayaquil. Up to 40 campaigners paraded through the streets of Ecuador's biggest city to the electoral council offices ahead of the vote. The four-legged mammal, which has been given the inventive nickname 'Mr Donkey', was dressed in a smart tie as he led his drum-banging supporters through the city. Despite voters superimposing the animals head on a man in a mock registration card, the donkey was refused entry to the building. This is very disturbing as I believe Mr Donkey would have little difficulty being elected to the council chambers in any town or city throughout the UK. I am thinking of starting a campaign to get Mr Donkey over here and running his campaign for office!

TUESDAY 20TH NOVEMBER 2012

A man has been taken to court for feeding police horses sausage rolls, after he tried to feed them to police horses 'who looked hungry'. Francis Kelly was arrested for trying to share the pastries with the animals because police didn't want the horses to eat them. Prosecutors claim the 41-year-old became 'threatening and abusive' when mounted officers ordered him to put the sausage rolls away. He is set to stand trial after pleading not guilty to a breach of the peace charge yesterday. The alleged incident happened in September 2012 and Mr Kelly will be back at the city's magistrates' court in February to plead his case a very serious offence indeed and one which should take precedent over any muggings, rapes and murders! In another case of horseplay, in 2005, Oxford University student Sam Brown was arrested after telling a police officer: 'Excuse me, do you realise your horse is gay?' The case was later dropped. (As reported previously in D J Wayne's blog)

WEDNESDAY 21ST NOVEMBER 2012

Customer services may not always be the best working environment to be in, whether it is face to face or even contact via telephone. As stated previously, there are those individuals who are rude and obnoxious just because they can be! Here is a great example:-

DVLA: "Thank you for calling today, how can I help you?"
Caller: "I need a driver's licence."
DVLA: "Okay, you can come to our office; as it is Saturday, we are open until 12:30 pm."
Caller: "I can't make it in time, can you fax me one?"
DVLA: "Sorry, sir. It's a plastic card and it cannot be faxed or emailed. We also have to take your photo, so this can be done only in person."
DVLA: "It was my birthday yesterday, so my licence is expired. Can't you do it over the phone?"
DVLA: "Sorry, sir, I cannot send you a plastic licence over the phone."
Caller: "F**k you!"
DVLA: "Sorry, sir. I can't do that over the phone, either.

THURSDAY 22ND NOVEMBER 2012

It makes my blood boil, it really does. It is one law for one and another law for others! What am I referring two? The ignorant, self-importance couldn't care less, unlawful, pathetic excuses for the so called traveller, and one in particular. We booked our tickets to see the legend that is Chris Barber, with his Jazz band at the Key Theatre in Peterborough. There is a public car park opposite the theatre to be used by the theatre goers, and it was getting quite full by the time we arrived there. Right in the middle of the car park there was a traveller's caravan and vehicle parked across not one but ACROSS five car parking spaces. The generator was in another. How did I know they were travellers? Because of the waste rubbish and bits of metal which surrounded the caravan! If law abiding people like me were even one minute late arriving back in the car park we would have a £30 fine and chased to pay it. The travellers are illegally parked and according to the receptionist in the theatre have been there for up to two weeks. The police and council officials have been called but they are a damp squid and unable to move these individuals away. There is only one answer, the individuals should be fined for illegal parking and summoned for fly tipping. If they will not pay up the caravan should be impounded, compress it into a two foot square block and drop it in the ocean. They will not park illegally again!!!

FRIDAY 23RD NOVEMBER 2012

Oh here we go again; apparently the UK Government has been paying Rwanda up to £21m in aid. Rwanda is a country in a permanent state of war with its neighbours. It is a country where millions of innocent people have perished. There is only one law, the law of the corrupt government. Rwanda has a role in the current conflict within the Democratic Republic of Congo and the UK government has now decided not to release a payment worth £21m. £16m was paid to Rwanda in September 2012 despite question marks over its alleged support for the M23 militia in DR Congo. The government also said it would give a further £18m for immediate humanitarian needs in the DR Congo.

International Development Secretary Justine Greening said £21m, which was due to be handed over to Rwanda next month, would not be released because President Paul Kagame's regime had breached agreements. Am I the only one who did not know we, the UK tax payers were subsidising this corrupt government. Am I the only one who objects to these payments while many families within this country are heading towards poverty with rents, food, petrol and the cost of heating increases in price every day?

Whilst I agree it is disgusting and a slight on mankind that Rwanda is in a permanent state of war and poverty it is not my fault. We do what we can for charity but the UK tax payers cannot save the world. Seafordsurf Radio cannot save the world, but it provides damn good free entertainment!!

SATURDAY 24TH NOVEMBER 2012

Questions: What does "Road closed ahead" mean? What can "Dangerous flooding ahead, no access" be interpreted as? Can "Flooding ahead – danger" be deciphered as? Apparently all three questions have one common answer: "Drive your vehicle around the barriers, disregard all warning signs, get your feet wet, get marooned and call out the emergency services" A number of vehicle drivers have attempted to manoeuvre through the flood waters in Whittlesey where the River Nene has broken its banks and caused havoc for motorists, and will continue to do so for a further few weeks. These drivers are a hazard to themselves and for others and even put the emergency services at risk. Police have issued on the spot fines to any motorists caught moving "road closed barriers" which may prevent others from acting stupid. Perhaps these drivers are a bit wet behind the ears, enjoy listening to Handel's Water Music, watch Oceans 11, enjoy Rugby Union (Leicester Tigers Toby Flood), or just plain stupid. I will go for the latter!!

SUNDAY 25TH NOVEMBER 2012

Just read an interesting article in the press and one which I need to put on my pre-retirement "bucket list". It has reminded me that anyone aged 75 and over can apply for a free TV licence. Now this is a bit of a dichotomy for me as I fully understand that revenue from the TV licence payers is the only form of income for Aunty Beeb. But 75, who picked that number out of a hat when the suggestion was made in a brainstorming session? Why not earlier? I will tell you why! After all if you were to be promoted to the position of Chairman of the BBC Trust and resign after 54 days when the job got tough you would receive a payoff of £450,000. That money has got to come from somewhere, and the only form of revenue is, yes you guessed it, the TV licence payers. There is only one answer to enable the BBC to waste money in payoffs and continue paying their megastars, who have their heads up their arses, exorbitant salaries. Raise the age of free TV licences to one hundred and ten. That should sort it!

MONDAY 27TH NOVEMBER 2012

What would you do if you were offered £10,000 to spend on whatever you liked? Pay off your outstanding bills, pay some of your mortgage off, purchase essentials, maybe purchase a new car, or even share it with the local community! The list is of course endless, depending on your own unique circumstances. But what about the community, what could £10K be used for, for the benefit of the community for all? Assisting the elderly with essential food and heating? Perhaps a contribution to the local youth club or pre-school activity centres. Or a road sign! The highways agency, which is funded by the taxpayer, has installed one road sign in the village of Thorney Toll at a cost of £10,000.

They justify the cost and break it down to justify it to us who know nothing. £2400 to purchase and install! £7600 for the design, survey work and safety audit. Forgive me for stating the bleeding obvious but how can anyone on this planet justify £7600 for a design which is just the same as any sign pointing to the village hall? Survey work: Some oik pointing to a spot and say "stick it there." Safety? Got me on that one! This is a blatant waste of public funds, and if this is the same up and down the country we could save enough money for us all to retire, or give it to some country in aid which means we are funding a corrupt government. Oh to be in politics!

WEDNESDAY 28TH NOVEMBER 2012

The next time you visit your local supermarket make sure you carry your ID with you. After all you may need it to prove your age if you wish to purchase alcohol and cigarettes. No problem there of course, I would consider it an honour, and welcome, to be asked for proof of age these days. Razor blades, knives, matches, glue and aerosol cans are on the "may I see proof of age" list.

However, the proof is in the pudding: one shopper Robert Nemeti was stunned when he was asked for ID as the dessert he was purchasing posed a risk to the roof of his mouth. Mr. Nemeti, 24, was going through the self-service checkout when an on-screen warning announced that his purchase had to be 'approved'.

A member of staff at the store in Southampton hurried over and asked Mr. Nemeti to produce identification.

When asked why, the female assistant told him that the Cadbury Hot Chocolate Pudding would get hot when cooked and may burn him. The member of staff demanded Mr. Nemeti produce identification showing he was over 18. Mr. Nemeti did manage to cook and eat the dessert that evening without injury.

THURSDAY 29TH NOVEMBER 2012

What is wrong with this coalition government and the labour opposition? There is allegedly a housing shortage in this country, but if you have read previous blogs of mine you would have read the solutions for this problem. We do not need to build on green belt land, remember this is a green and pleasant land and that should be protected at all costs. Fight against the greedy fat cat developers, fight against councillors who happen to be in the planning and building departments and above all fight against unopposed immigration.

In the news today in black and white, "Migrants fuel need for green belt homes". That is the reason officials are talking of relaxing the rules on planning applications. Not for our own people but for individuals coming from other countries, stop this lunacy now. Write to your MP, unless he or her has been up late fiddling his or hers expenses. Write to your local councillor, unless they are busy planning the next town to be situated in the middle of your school playing field. Don't wish to get in the way of our elected officials in their day to day job!!!

FRIDAY 30TH NOVEMBER 2012

D J Wayne's letter to the editor of Private Eye

Good evening, I am not a politician, councillor or a member of a political organisation. I am an ordinary British guy who is getting more and more disillusioned with councillors and politicians alike. They do not listen to the ordinary person and they do not see what is going on around therm. They are a blinkered racehorse, never mind the riots of last year I predict it will not be long before civil unrest is on the streets again, not by political groups but by ordinary working people. Why am I contacting Private Eye? Because you have balls to tell it how it is.

Update 1: The reply was "thank you for contacting Private Eye"

SATURDAY 1ST DECEMBER 2012

Why is it that when you may have to make a claim on your house insurance you are made to feel like a criminal? I unfortunately had a slight mishap with my laptop and thus decided to make a claim to my insurers who are a well-known branded name. It started off bad when the recorded message told me if I were to make a fraudulent claim or had knowledge of a fraudulent claim I would be expecting a long custodial sentence. I was also informed that all claims made by me would be recorded and sent to other agencies for their information. So much for data protection! Considering I have made two claims in thirty years with the same Building Society I thought that was quite a good track record. The laptop is only eighteen months old and I had it seen by a reputable high street store. It is un-repairable. The insurers have commissioned an external company to pick up the PC, make their own assessment and decide if it is repairable!! I doubt if it is even remotely repairable with a full glass of red wine spilt over the keyboard! And even if it was, how long would it last before the corrosion sets in?

Once they make their assessment, if I am eligible for a replacement, they will choose the models which will only be available from one supplier, how stupid is that! I do not want to purchase from this supplier! I feel I am being held to ransom and will be palmed off with a product I do not want.

Watch this space!

Update 1: The claim has been a total shambles from the second I reported the issue. It was dealt with by individuals who did not possess the basic skills and there was nobody at all willing to take responsibility and drive home a solution which was agreeable to all parties. I received a replacement which crashed within a week only to be replaced by the same model. Would you want that? I think not. It has been shambolic and to date I have not received any correspondence from the insurance company and due to legal reasons I am unable to confirm or deny it was Nationwide!

Update 2: I have received a replacement, replacement, laptop computer and after three weeks it crashed with exactly the same critical error message being displayed. The insurance company has finally agreed to a cash settlement to enable me to purchase a replacement from a reputable retailer of my choice. To date I am still waiting for the settlement to arrive and I live in hope!

Update 3: It is now Saturday 15th March 2013 and I am still waiting for a cheque with the agreed amount to settle the case. It has now been three long months without a computer.

Update 4: Saturday 23rd March 2013. The long awaited cheque has finally arrived, nearly four months after the initial incident. I can honestly say this has been one of the worst experiences ever. If this is an example of how the country runs then I am not a bit surprised we are a total mess bogged down with red tape and officialdom!

SUNDAY 2ND DECEMBER 2012

It is that awful feeling when you are in the garden picking up what the dogs have left that you know that the bottom of your shoe does not feel the same! With dark mornings and dark evenings undertaking this task is like plotting your way through a minefield.

Armed with a small torch you try to pick out little shadows here and there as you place one foot in front of the other and move steadily forward, but also looking left and right in order to spot any changes in the landscape. This is a tricky maneuver and when your foot comes down, not on gravel, but another substance, you know, you just know the move was in vain and a change of tactics is required.

MONDAY 3RD DECEMBER 2012

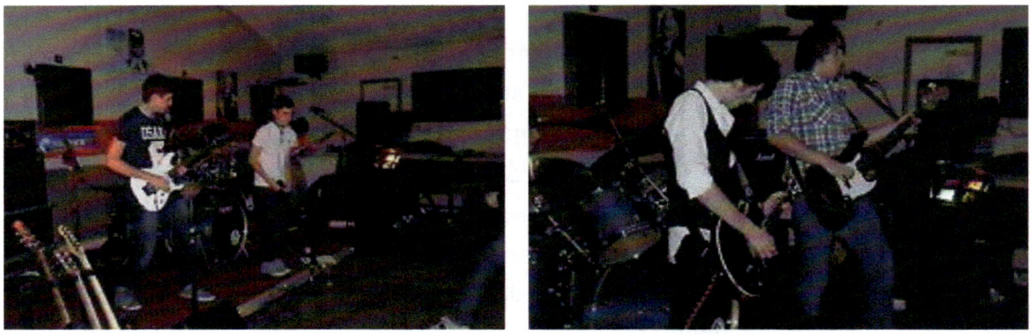

Whittlesey HAS got talent. The final was between Alice, Jeanie, Rocket Jump and Amplified. The live show has been recorded and will be re-broadcast on SSR **www.seafordsurfradio.com**. email dj@seafordsurfradio.com for details and timings.

TUESDAY 4TH DECEMBER 2012

How superb are our British Pubs? In light of the fact that this and previous governments wish to destroy the English heritage, the majority are excellent and should be saved at all costs. With ever increasing rents, rates, brewery price increases not to mention extortionist gas and electricity prices dozens of public houses are closing every week.

The government does not seem to give a damn and seem to welcome demolition to be replaced by "affordable" homes or yuppie pads. The English pub is a haven where friends and strangers can meet up in a neutral environment and put the world to rights without having to resort to bombs and all-out war. In fact the government sitting MPs could learn a lot in this environment although they do a damn good job of talking rubbish most of the time anyway, and fiddling their expenses in private. Well I am off down the pub for a good English pint and a chat, whilst it is still there!

WEDNESDAY 5TH DECEMBER 2012

We British love our seaside saucy postcards and innuendoes and there is nothing quite as funny as a penis. But a recent news story in the Metro probably confirms the British are the only nation who can "ave a damn good laff" A cartoon penis drawn on a blackboard has caused outrage in Slovakia after the rude image was unintentionally broadcast to the nation. The school boy humour failed to raise a smile from a selection of disgruntled viewers who were less than amused by the prank.

Head teacher Maria Franikova was being interviewed in her classroom at a school in Poltar, Slovakia, about an upcoming strike. While the programme's editors failed to spot the cheeky chalk drawing lurking in the background, featuring a man with a penis as a nose, eagle-eyed viewers did. The TV station only realised its mistake after its switchboard was inundated with a raft of complaints from angry viewers complaining about the image. One angry viewer Miroslav Spak, said: 'I don't know whether this was a secret message from the teachers to the government or whoever, but it should have been wiped off the board. 'There are enough d***heads in politics without creating more,' he added. Now I CAN relate to that last statement perhaps that is universal!!

THURSDAY 6TH DECEMBER 2012

Now I, like most of the nation, have come to terms with prancing about on the dance floor to a crazy Korean PSY performing "gangham style dance". After all you need to do is to perform sexual innuendoes and ride a horse, oh and lasso the lady in front of you. That's the dance for me! However I am not too sure about the latest craze which is hitting the headlines. Forget milking (now that one did pass me by) porting is the latest internet craze set to sweep the nation, and it's going to drive mums and dads everywhere absolutely potty. It has begun with students at Durham University dressed in suits pouring bottles of port over their heads (thus ruining perfectly good clean white shirts) before uploading the clips onto YouTube. Last month, undergraduates from a Newcastle university hit the headlines after a video of them throwing four-pint containers of milk over themselves in public places went viral. However the Durham students have taunted their 'student cousins' saying: 'We figure if you're going to do something you might as well do it properly. 'Don't cry over spilt milk Newcastle – do it the Durham way! Porting is set to take on milking. 'It's all about one-upmanship,' a porting spokesman said. One-upmanship it may be but I call it a damn waste of a good porter, and oh if you wish me to get going on a rant, a waste of student money. I thought students were supposed to be poor? I think I will stick with PSY!

FRIDAY 7TH DECEMBER 2012

Why does black ivory coffee taste so good? Because it comes out of an elephant's rear end, that's why. Well Starbucks have been in the news recently for apparently not paying any or very little corporation tax for the past few years. Now, with Starbucks sort of admitting they were wrong have made a complete arse of themselves. Which brings me very nicely into the latest news about a new brew which is one of the most expensive in the world at £30 a cup, as every bean used to make it has to be plucked out of a pile of elephant dung. Producers in Thailand say feeding the ingredients to their herd of 20 elephants improves the flavour, as the animals' stomach acid makes them less bitter.

The coffee, dubbed crap-uccino has already become the butt of jokes. But it seems Canadian Blake Dinkin, who has spent £300,000 developing the idea, may have the last laugh. The first 70kg batch of coffee he produced in northern Thailand has sold out. "There's definitely something wild about it that I can't put a name on," said US tourist Ryan Nelson, 31, after trying it at a hotel near the elephants' home. Now, I am neither a coffee drinker, nor tea actually, but can you imagine the troubles of sifting through elephant dung for those tea leaves? No I will pass on that and continue with my water and lemon juice!

SATURDAY 8TH DECEMBER 2012

I am not too sure about this. If you remember I blogged about the naked rambler who has been in and out of prison fighting for his right to ramble in the altogether, well Andrew Lyall Pointon was arrested in August 2011 when a woman reported him to authorities after spotting him running naked, while wearing a pair of trainers. The 47-year-old was detained three days later when he emerged from one of his naked runs near Tauranga. The woman was apparently so shaken by the event she promised never to return to the Oropi Bike Park. Now this always amazes me why a swinging todger and a pair of balls actually frightens people, after all fifty per cent of the world have them! But her disgust did not prevent Justice Paul Heath from upholding Mr Pointon's appeal against his conviction for offensive behaviour at Tauranga High Court. "If it was offensive then God wouldn't have given us genitals," the jogger told the Dominion Post. Good point! However we do a lot of walking and I do prefer the thermals than the birthday suit, each to their own I suppose, after all people have fought and died for a free world!

SUNDAY 9TH DECEMBER 2012

Sunday 9th December. Well the day started off well so we thought we would walk across the Delph to see the flood damage for ourselves. With the river road closed it takes two hours to get from Whittlesey to Peterborough and the same time on the return journey.

These pictures show the extent of the flooding. Not sure about the tree log in the jeep I reckon that was human!

MONDAY 10TH DECEMBER 2012

It is always interesting finding out what goes on in other parts of the ever shrinking globe. A Ukrainian man is giving people the chance to lie down in a coffin - to prepare themselves for the afterlife. Now this is fine but I do not really wish to visit the afterlife just yet, so count me out on the prep for this one. Stepan Piryanyk, from Truskavets, who has been making coffins for more than a decade, calls his new service 'coffin therapy'. It gives people the chance to lie inside a casket for approximately 15 minutes - putting the lid on is optional. Whoa just there for a second have you ever had that dream where you are buried alive in a coffin? Scary or what, I could never go and see that film where the leading man spent most of the 2 hour film underground! Mr. Piryanyk explained: "When you lay in the coffin, it feels just like a bed. It's the same sheets; the same pillow... a wooden coffin has its own aura inside." There you go then not enough room for me and my aura! The businessman has a room set up for his customers with several empty coffins to choose from, clients can recline as a soundtrack of birdsong and water falling plays in the background. Client Anna Petrukhina, 51, said: "After a hard working day you can come in and just relax - it's great. You go home in a completely different mood." I reckon he must be in a "dead end" job! Nope I'm sorry this particular Ukrainian past time is not for me.

TUESDAY 11TH DECEMBER 2012

As a regular reader of DJ Wayne's daily blog you may get an idea of what would be in my manifesto if I were in a political party, which I am not! I believe I am not backward in coming forward and make comments on subjects which the ordinary working people of the UK are maybe thinking the same way. I disagree with the immigration policy which is a farce, sentencing of criminals by judges who are still working at 100 years of age and the laughable sentences awarded. You can get a prison sentence for not mowing your lawn but get a £10 fine for committing murder. Unemployed foreigners get free housing and benefits and get paid a vast sum for each offspring they produce. Well I suppose they need to do something in their spare time! However we could learn from a judge in the US who ordered a man with nine children to stop procreating until he can afford to pay for them. Corey Curtis, 44, of Racine, Wisconsin, was told to stop breeding as a condition of probation until he can financially support his nine children from six different women. Racine County Judge Tim Boyle sentenced Curtis to the rare punishment as a condition of a three-year probation order for failing to pay $50,000 in child support, plus another $40,000 in interest. "Common sense dictates you shouldn't have kids you can't afford," Judge Boyle said. "I will make that a condition of the probation." Well it is a start I suppose and there is always "bobbit" to finish off!! A little harsh maybe but let the working tax payers have the last vote on that one!

WEDNESDAY 12TH DECEMBER 2012

I am always annoyed when the UK government is giving away UK taxpayers money especially when we have high taxation, high VAT and extortionate prices at the petrol pumps. Now we find out we are contributing £2.2m to a Libyan dissident and his family who say MI6 was involved in their illegal rendition. If it was illegal and bear in mind that MI6 is there to protect us the general public then there must have been a reason why the actions took place. The individual involved has said "My children will now have the chance to complete their education in the new, free Libya."I will be able to afford the medical care I need because of the injuries I suffered in prison. Well good for you, it is always good to know that I am contributing to your children's education that really does make me feel better. If there is anything else I can do please let me know and I will try my best to oblige. A second man, Abdul Hakim Belhaj, is continuing with a similar legal action against the British government. The floodgates have opened up; don't bank on the price of petrol going down!

THURSDAY 13TH DECEMBER 2012

I have not commented on the case of the hoax call which resulted in the death of a nurse as it is so terrible and beyond belief. Jacintha Saldanha was found dead in her nurses' quarters on Friday, three days after the call from Australian radio presenters pretending to be the Queen and Prince Charles. None of us can really appreciate what went through her mind to take such drastic action. Perhaps the radio DJs should be suspended and sent for trial for manslaughter, perhaps not? Perhaps they should be reprimanded for their foolish actions, perhaps not? Pranks like this go on every day, some are really funny and make people laugh or have a degree of shock and either way it is entertainment. We hear it on BBC radio and see it on the television. We have to make a judgment between entertainment and infringement of privacy and that I am sure will be a thin red line.

FRIDAY 14TH DECEMBER 2012

What do Pinkie, Killiecrankie, Philiphaugh, Prestonpans and Sheriffmuir have in common with that fantastic movie The 39 steps? Not a lot you may say but there is a link between the Scottish names and the movie. Here is the link: Thirty-nine sites of violent clashes on Scottish soil have been officially recognised in Scotland's Inventory of Historic Battlefields and those names mentioned have been included in the list. I am all in favour with preserving the last traces of historical events that shaped the nation of Scotland even if most of them were against the English. This is how our nations have been shaped throughout our glorious history. Highlights include Dunbar I (1296) in East Lothian, which marked the first battle of the Scottish Wars of Independence. Dunkeld (1689) in Perth and Kinross saw house-to-house fighting between Jacobite and government forces. Loudon Hill (1307) in East Ayrshire marked one of Robert the Bruce's first victories over English troops. It is important to remember these events between Scotland and England just as importantly we must remember how Scotland and England have stood, fought and died shoulder to shoulder fighting in numerous wars and skirmishes against tyrants and despots. I ask all Scottish people to remember this when the lunacy of independence raises its ugly head in the future. We reside in Great Britain, the union, share a union flag, we are one. Independence will drive a wedge between us and let the dogs of war ruin us both. Think about it!

SATURDAY 15TH DECEMBER 2012

Newtown

Connecticut

Children 20

Boys 12

Girls 8

Adults 6

Ages 6 & 7

British 1

Gunman 1

Why??

SUNDAY 16TH DECEMBER 2012

It is always a sad day when we lose a little of our heritage, and that is what we have lost with the closure of Hereford Racecourse. Its final meeting was Sunday 16th December 2012. More than 80 horses competed in seven races. Owners Arena Leisure and Northern Racing said the current 17-year lease made it difficult to invest in the racecourse, which was leased from Herefordshire Council. The market share of horse racing has diminished over the past 10 years with the rise of internet betting. For the connoisseurs of the sport Hereford was a right-handed track approximately a mile-and-a-half in circumference with nine fences including two open ditches. Horse racing has been taking place in Hereford since August 1771 and it was at this course along with Catterick that I personally learnt the craft of betting whilst serving in the Royal signals. You don't go to race courses to make a fortune of course but you can have a great day out and maybe just maybe at the end of the day break even before going to the local curry house for the dish of the day and a few beers. Ah to serve your country!

MONDAY 17TH DECEMBER 2012

In previous blogs I have stated that we do not need wholesale building of houses in this country. There is no need to build houses especially on prime agricultural land. It is stupid which is also what many councillors are. When it comes to decision making they have not been on the course and been presented with the certificate of competence. Farmers concerned about plans to sell off their land to build an energy park have handed a hamper full of their produce to council leaders. The gesture was made to show bosses the products they would be stopped from making for the public, if the farms in and around Newborough are sold off by the council. The hamper contained bread, potatoes, peas, flour, oats, carrots, malt and rape seed oil among other items. One opponent said, "Not only will vital foods be stopped from being made, we believe this scheme is too expensive and will bankrupt the city of Peterborough in the future." Councillor David Harrington, who opposes the plans, added: "The hamper shows how much local produce will be lost if this goes ahead." A good protest indeed but will the greedy misguided councillors get the message? I think not!

TUESDAY 18TH DECEMBER 2012

Have you had your recommended five portions today? Be careful, they could prove to be dangerous, if not life threatening. A man was hospitalised after overdosing on Brussels sprouts, it has emerged. The Scottish resident from Ayrshire was rushed to hospital after eating a plateful of the festive vegetables. What caused this to happen? Brussels sprouts are rich in vitamin K, a chemical the body uses to promote blood clotting. The man, who has not been named, suffered a heart failure after the sprouts interfered with his blood thinning medication. Doctors at Golden Jubilee National Hospital in Clydebank, West Dunbartonshire, were left stumped by his condition before learning of his above-average Brussels sprout intake. Consultant cardiologist Dr Roy Gardner said: 'Patients who are taking anticoagulants are generally advised not to eat too many green leafy vegetables, as they are full of vitamin K, which antagonise the action of this vital medication.' It gives diners not so keen on sprouts another reason to pass on the unpopular vegetable when offered a helping on Christmas Day.

WEDNESDAY 19TH DECEMBER 2012

What do horse manure and urine, straw, 8 pineapples and £10,000 have in common? Keep thinking! Keep thinking! Got it? Pineapples, grown using Victorian gardening methods which includes horse manure, urine and straw is so luxurious a price tag of £10,000 has been placed on them. The luxurious crop was matured at Cornwall's Lost Gardens of Heligan and is one of eight pineapples, each costing £1,200 to grow, that are ready to eat. But anyone who does plan bidding for the £10,000 pineapple will be disappointed as staff at the complex are planning on keeping the special fruit all to themselves. A spokesman at the Lost Gardens said, "The high cost produce had explosive flavour and was deliciously sweet. We'd use about 90 tonnes of manure over the course of year which isn't cheap to source and transport,' he said. Enough said!

THURSDAY 20TH DECEMBER 2012

The Mayan calendar predicts the world, as we know it, will expire on December 21st. So make sure you have got some ways through your bucket list before it happens. However residents in a town in Poland have been literally living in the end of the world for as long as they care to remember. Now, the locals at the settlement in Poland named "End of the World" are probably hoping it does all finish after continually having their signposts stolen by apocalypse believers. Residents of Koniec Swiata have accused outsiders, who believe the Mayan prophecy, of taking the signage and making their daily lives difficult. "Our name means literally End Of The World, so once the doomsday hunters found this out they wouldn't leave us alone," said 50-year-old local Roman Adamus. A local 85 year old said, "I've lived here all my life and these people are a bloody nightmare. Hopefully they'll leave us alone if the world doesn't end. Watch this space.

FRIDAY 21ST DECEMBER 2012

Well, it has finally arrived!
Correct date – check

Ticked what I could on my bucket list – check
Stuff paying the mortgage – check
Quit job and did a very naughty thing with the maid – check

Today is the day so I will apologise now as this will be my final entry in my blog! One in 10 of us are said to be as anxious as I am as today marks the end of the world. The Ancient Mayans predicted this doomsday. That the world will end in 2012 is the most widely-disseminated doomsday tale in human history. Recent hurricanes, unrest in the Middle East, solar flares, mystery planets about to collide with us - all "proof" of what the ancient Mayans knew would come to pass on 21 December 2012. The "Long Count" cycle of the Mayan calendar began in 3114 BCE and is widely accepted to end on 21/12/12 CE. In 3114 BCE the calendar reset to zero with the turning of the 13th bak'tun (which is a smaller, 400 year cycle). This time, however, it does not reset to zero but merely goes on to the 14th bak'tun. So, there we have it then, the technical bits, quite interesting really, pity I will not be able to share it with friends down the pub tomorrow!

SATURDAY 22ND DECEMBER 2012

Morning fellow bloggers D J Wayne here.

Day after the end of the world - Check
Refresh bucket list – check
Ring the Bank, apologise profusely, and pay outstanding debt – check
Contact work and confirm there has been a misunderstanding and crawl - Check
The maid, come back to you on that one!! Check

Well, the world did not end, well not in the literacy sense anyway. It did end of course, it ended one cycle to begin another not that we may have seen it of course. After all as we go on our daily way we tend not to see what is happening around us. We are in our own little bubble, yet there is no snow moving around as the bubble gets shaken by the gremlin. Our lives are once again in organised turmoil awaiting the next prediction to come along! D J Wayne's blog is once again back tomorrow

SUNDAY 23RD DECEMBER 2012

There are fads and there are crazes, they come and they go, some need to go before they arrive! A bit like gangham really. We have recently had "milking" and "portering" so how about "frosting"? The weird new pastime involves members of the public dressing like they were going to the beach in the middle of July, even though they are actually in freezing temperatures and covered in snow. Users have posted pictures of themselves on the Frosters Anonymous page dressed in Speedos, shorts and bathing suits. The trend, which started in Montana, US, also sees some daring souls plant their heads in the snow, play games and go totally naked in a protest against the cold weather. Participants are encouraged to recreate their most loved summer pursuits, with some deciding to pretend to swim in the snow and play a round of golf. Frosting has become so popular that it has been taken up all around the world, including places in Eastern Europe where it's freezing almost all year round. Any volunteers? Onzee and hot water bottle for me!!

MONDAY 24TH DECEMBER 2012

Great News! Santa Claus has completed his delivery of presents across the world - and is now set to rest back at the North Pole for another year. Children around the world had been kept up to date about his progress thanks to Norad - an organisation that provides aerospace warning information to the US and Canada. The organisation's Norad Tracks Santa site provided up-to-date information on the progress of Father Christmas and his reindeer - Dasher, Dancer, Prancer, Vixen, Comet, Cupid, Donner, Blitzen and Rudolph. Norad Tracks Santa uses radar, satellites and high-speed digital "Santa Cams" that have been pre-positioned at many locations around the world. The cameras capture images and videos of Santa and his reindeer as they make their journey each Christmas Eve. Canadian and US fighter jets are even used to escort Santa and his sleigh through North American airspace - presumably to allay any elf and safety fears his visit might provoke.

Santa usually starts his journey at the International Date Line in the Pacific Ocean and travels west, meaning he visits the South Pacific first, then New Zealand and Australia. After that, he flies up to Japan, over to Asia, across to Africa, then onto Western Europe, Canada, the United States, Mexico and Central and South America. The journey can be followed on video. To calm any doubters, Norad has sought to answer the age-old question "is there a Santa Clause?" It said: "Mountains of historical data and more than 50 years of Norad tracking information leads us to believe that Santa Claus is alive and well in the hearts of people throughout the world." Thank you Santa!

TUESDAY 25TH DECEMBER 2012

Merry Christmas bloggers! I really do hope you have a good one and you receive all the presents and gifts you have wished for. However Christmas is for giving not receiving. Forget about all the adverts on the radio and TV. We do not need all those things. We do not need the hype and the credit card bill for the next 12 months. What we do need is peace on earth and good will towards mankind. Heard that somewhere before, now where was it? Is it too much to ask for? Apparently so, but keep praying to your God for it anyway. It really could work. Merry Christmas everybody, merry Christmas

WEDNESDAY 26TH DECEMBER 2012

I am really not sure about this and I am unclear about what we, as individual members of society, should be focusing on. The Pyramid Centre in North Bretton Peterborough has been made the subject of a dispersal order in a bid to tackle anti-social and rowdy behaviour. The Anti-social Behaviour Act 2003 came into force on Christmas Eve and will remain for six months. In 2012 so far, there have been more than 75 reports of crime and anti-social behaviour in the area, including nuisance and abusive youths, criminal damage, arson and hoax calls to emergency services. Officers and PCSOs can use the powers when there are reasonable grounds for believing that the presence or behaviour of a group of two or more people in a public place has resulted, or is likely to result, in members of the public being intimidated, harassed, alarmed or distressed.

The group can be told to disperse and leave the location for a specified length of time, but not for more than 24 hours, and failing to comply can result in arrest. In the first place why do these unruly youths gather at this place? Secondly why are they intent on vandalism and thirdly will they really take any notice of the order, after all they will be back after 24hours probably after harassing another part of town. No I am not convinced, there has to be a better way in improving the lives of the residents and the youths for them to be good contributors of society and respectable part of the community in which they live!

THURSDAY 27TH DECEMBER 2012

Entries are being taken for the Whittlesey Citizenship Award recognising those aged over 16 and who have helped others and live in Whittlesey, Coates, Eastrea, Turves or Pondersbridge. Do I qualify? Well I am definitely over the age of 16! I reside in the hamlet of Turves. My good deeds, I nearly assisted a Ukrainian lorry driver who was lost. It was seven in the morning when I took our two dogs out for their early morning walk. It was pitch black and of course raining. Before slowing down in front of me the lorry managed to splash me not once but twice before coming to a halt. The driver jumped out and pointed to a soggy piece of paper.

"You know, yes?" he asked. I looked at the water stained delivery address, "I know no!" I replied "yes you know, burnthoos siddings yes" he was very stern with me. I looked again at the delivery address on the blotting paper, "Burnthouse Sidings". Well we were standing getting drenched on Burnthouse Road, but the sidings I was unaware of. "No, sorry I said and commenced to walk off". I am sure at this point he kicked some mud at me and swore, but I cannot confirm that of course. I can confirm six heavy duty wheels splashed me as he made his way down the road! Oh, and I can also confirm I helped a hedgehog across the road one evening. Unfortunately it appears he was going in the opposite direction and never made it, if that was the same one I saw in the morning? Nomination envelopes should be marked "Whittlesey Citizenship Awards" and sent to Susan Evans, Whittlesey Town Council, Grosvenor Road, Whittlesey, PE7 1AQ by February 28.

FRIDAY 28TH DECEMBER 2012

Here we go then; London Underground (LU) station cleaners will begin a 48-hour strike, in a dispute over pay, on New Year eve. RMT's general secretary Bob Crow said the cleaners were doing "some of the dirtiest jobs" on minimum pay. Well what makes these individuals so special then? It is a cleaning job like thousands of other cleaning jobs around the UK on minimum wage. Most of them are grateful and take their hard earned money home to help pay the rent and feed their children. Obviously the London Underground cleaners get paid too much as they can afford to lose two days' pay whilst others struggle. If they do not wish to do the job they are contracted to do then there are thousands of replacements. This strike will do only one thing, yet again bring a little misery to the thousands of rail users who expect to complete their journey in some state of cleanliness. It is the cleaners who stink!

SATURDAY 29TH DECEMBER 2012

How could I have nearly missed this one? A number of London Underground drivers have gone on strike in a long-running row over bank holiday pay. Large parts of the service have been disrupted as a result of the Boxing Day strike and more buses were brought in. Members of the Aslef union have walked out for 24 hours from after voting 9-1 in favour of strike action. How many voted 10?

This again, is a prime example of kicking in the teeth of the very people who pay their wages. It is scandalous that a few money grabbing individuals can disrupt the travel arrangements of the very people they should be providing a service for. It is the third successive walkout by Tube drivers on what is the first day of the post-Christmas sales.

Still look on the bright side, there will be loads of overtime whist the rolling stock gets to the correct location. Ah these drivers know how to bring home the bacon! Unless you are in Golders Green of course! Great job girls and boys!

SUNDAY 30TH DECEMBER 2012

Sashes, tiaras, revealing swimwear, hair extensions and "I want world peace and wars to end, oh and I do charity work in my spare time", yes the beauty contest is upon us. Love it or hate it, it is just compulsive viewing, although the heyday has long since passed. But this one takes the biscuit, because all the contestants are elephants. Well I have seen a few dogs in my time, but elephants? Ninety elephants and their mahouts (handlers) entered the contest, part of Nepal's elephant festival, in Chitwan national park. Contestants were assessed on their decorations, including headdresses and painted toenails, with just three making it through to the final. I bet they were in front of the mirrors for ages working on their speeches. Can you see the elephant in the room?

MONDAY 31TH DECEMBER 2012

Remember the Oompa Loompas? They were the little people working in the chocolate factory. I thought it very strange then and recent activities have made me even more suspicious. Police are seeking two Oompa Loompas in connection with an assault in a Norwich street. A group of four are thought to have attacked a man in the early hours of Thursday December 27. Norfolk police said the 28-year-old victim was attacked as he left a kebab shop next to Tesco in Prince of Wales Road. The victim sustained a cut below his right eye, two black eyes and cuts to his nose and lips. Anyone who witnessed the incident or has knowledge of it should contact Crimestoppers anonymously on 0800 555111. Enough said!

TUESDAY 1ST JANUARY 2013

Happy New Year from DJ Wayne and everyone at Seafordsurf Radio. 2013 is going to be awesome and we have so much planned for you all this year. Never mind the Fiscal Cliff, although they are a great band I must admit. If Professor Hawkins can get a gig on Go Compare then SSR can rule the world. Follow us on our home page, live message board, twitter, facebook and of course our daily blog. May your God go with you! Peace and love to you all!

WEDNESDAY 2ND JANUARY 2013

Are you suffering from the holiday blues? And suffering from "over indulgence?" Is one of your new year's resolutions the commitment to try a new diet? Be careful though make sure you choose the right one for you. For example you could try the "Chew and spit" thought up by American, Horace Fletcher, who decided a lot of chewing and spitting, was the way to lose weight. Fletcherism, as it was called, promoted chewing a mouthful of food until all "goodness" was extracted, then spitting out the fibrous material that was left.

No, not convinced? Then, how about the Tapeworm diet? Dieters would swallow beef tapeworm cysts, usually in the form of a pill. The theory was that the tapeworms would reach maturity in the intestines and absorb food. This could cause weight loss, along with diarrhoea and vomiting.

Still not convinced? Well how about the rubber diet from the mid-1800s. With the Industrial Revolution and mass production, suddenly the use of rubber expanded massively. That included rubber knickers and corsets. The thinking behind both was that rubber held in fat but more importantly caused sweating, hopefully leading to weight loss. They were worn by both men and women, but not much fun as the skin-macerating underwear meant flesh would be softened and broken down by extended exposure to moisture, making it vulnerable to infection. Well, I am off for a burger and a pint then, and I intend to chew and swallow every mouthful!

THURSDAY 3RD JANUARY 2013

While the country is going through its austerity measures and cutbacks it is always gratifying to know that the government, the very people who installed the measures are doing their bit. For instance rail minister Simon Burns. Now Mr Burns, the rail minister uses a chauffeur-driven car to go to work instead of the train. Good for the geese and gander springs to mind!

The alleged cost to the taxpayer £80,000 a year. Great value indeed! The chauffeur driven vehicle takes him from his home in Chelmsford, where he is MP, to Westminster, a distance of 35 miles. Now that is really taking the p**s out of rail commuters who pay upward of £5,000 for their season ticket. The minister has no morals, as is the case of many government ministers, officials and Councillors. I hear their next slogan is "Vote for me and I will take you for a ride!"

FRIDAY 4TH JANUARY 2013

Well Christmas is over; the decorations have been taken down and put back into the loft to gather dust for another year. But what about the Christmas tree, no not the imitation tree, the real one which sheds its pines by the millions! There is only one solution; we need a Christmas tree throwing contest. Specifically the world Christmas tree throwing championships held in Germany. It is known as "Knut-Fest," and competitors are asked to bring along their old trees, stripped of lights and other decorations, and see how far they can throw them.

There are three disciplines in the competition; Weitwurf (javelin-style), Hammerwurf (hammer-style) and Hochwurf (high jump-style) throwing. The overall winner is decided by the total distance achieved over the course of the day. The current champion has thrown a total distance of 22.45 metres over the three throwing disciplines. Sound great to me, well I am off for a bratwurst and chips and a bit of wellie wanging!

SATURDAY 5TH JANUARY 2013

Interesting article in the Telegraph today, "Council faces £10m black hole". Now regular readers of DJ Wayne's daily blog will know that I am not exactly a true fan of Councillors and other so called representatives of the general public. After all, they are our saviours the ones who demonstrate true dedication for the good of the land, with no reward for themselves!

Council leaders in Peterborough are battling to plug a £10m "black hole", in next year's budget, leading to fears over front-line cuts. Now I have to say these bleeding hearts Councillors are the very people who have mismanaged the books so you really have to feel sorry for them. So, what is to become of them? A recent TV advert springs to mind, the one with compare the market with Professor Hawkins. The same fate may be a "just deserts" for these Councillors!

SUNDAY 6TH JANUARY 2013

Bad drivers are in the news yet again, and not just in DJ Wayne's universal acclaimed daily blog. Bad driving seems to be the norm these days. Once these so called drivers get behind the wheel of their vehicle they turn in to animals who believe they own the roads and nobody else has the right to be in the same near vicinity as they are.

Vehicles with poor or no headlamps, speeding, no indicators and my pet hate tailgaters. Now there are other idiots who join the list. Those who jump red lights! Apparently it is more of a problem than any of us realise. In particular red light jumping is a problem at railway level crossings.

Why? So that these idiots on the road can save themselves two minutes, and in the process probably kill someone else. These individuals should not be allowed to get away with these actions. We have the pictures, take them to court, ban them from driving destroy their vehicles. There you go I have just saved a life!

MONDAY 7TH JANUARY 2013

You have heard of the black dog of the Fens and if you haven't then look it up, it is awesome. But this is the case of the "cuddly cat toy", which has sparked panther speculation. A large cuddly toy left on a grass bank triggered concerns that a black cat may be on the loose in Peterborough. Passers-by reported the feline as fears grew that the big black cat could be dangerous. The sightings rekindled speculation about the mythical "beast of Bretton" a large black cat reputedly sighted in city environs. So if you see a cuddly toy on the side of the road, it is only a tail to tell, and of course it is paws for thought! Of course it could be catastrophic if you ignored it but hey let's not pussy foot about!

TUESDAY 8TH JANUARY 2013

I am always very critical of the week and wishy washy awards given to criminals from the law courts. Every day we hear stories where the punishments do not fit the crime. So I am enlightened to read that there is evidence that the law courts have been reading extracts from D J Wayne's blog.

Today a car and van have been crushed after being used in fuel theft. The two vehicles were seized following a £6000 diesel theft at the brick-works at Kings Dyke Whittlesey. It followed the convictions of two individuals in relation to the theft. On this occasion I have to say well done and I hope others in authority read more of my blog!

WEDNESDAY 9TH JANUARY 2013

A friend of mine was looking at a poster on the works social notice board glancing over the excursions and offers for 2013 when one court her eye. She has always fancied going to Scotland and soaking up the atmosphere of our long history with our UK brethren (the same one which the Scottish National Party wish to destroy, but that is another story for another day.)

The poster advertised four days bed, breakfast and evening meal at a castle in Edinburgh which sounded exactly the Scottish experience she wished to be involved with. As she was making notes of the telephone number and contact name a colleague, who was Scottish passed by.

She inquired if he had been to Edinburgh? "Och eye", he replied, "but you dunna want to go there", he said. Puzzled, she asked why on earth not? He replied, "Coz it's full of English people", and walked off. The contact name and number is now torn up and in the bin. Elusions have been shattered!

THURSDAY 10TH JANUARY 2013

Tricky situation at work today and all to do with interpretations! In an office environment with different languages and dialects it is always possible to lose the original meaning of words, sentences and phrases. For instances as I was speaking with an associate, she mentioned that a colleague had been moaning and complaining all morning about her fanny eater. I asked if she could repeat what she had been complaining about. "Her fanny eater" she said again.

Well at this point I did not really wish to ask again, but I did. "Her fanny eater?" I inquired. The look of puzzlement on her face was fantastic. After a short pregnant pause she said, "no, not her fanny eater, her fan heater". Apparently it was not working when she came to work. Well, how was I to know?

FRIDAY 11TH JANUARY 2013

V

A "torrent of filth".

MP's called for it to be banned from the airwaves.

"The most sexually explicit language ever heard on television".

Conservative MP Sir Gerald Howarth attempted to get it band. But now confesses he had not read it in full when he made these comments - and had not realised it was about the desecration of a loving parents' grave.

V

V a poem by Tony Harrison was published in 1985 and is steeped in the politics of the time. The poem is prefaced by a quotation from Arthur Scargill, president of the National Union of Mineworkers and alludes to the recently-ended miners' strike:

V

"These Vs are all the versuses of life. From LEEDS v. DERBY, Black/White/and man v. Wife, Communist v. Fascist, Left v. Right.

V

Is a classic poem which highlights a number of subjects it is not politically correct to mention any more in this country of ours!

Read it, take it in, think about it and digest the content.

SATURDAY 12TH JANUARY 2013

A horse goes into a bar and the barman asks, "why the long face?" Horse DNA has been found in some beef burgers being sold in UK and Irish supermarkets. Now there is a surprise, I have often wondered what goes into the variety of "muck burgers" being sold in dodgy outlets in Peterborough.

Who knows what else is in them, badger, ferret, fox and dog food, although I must admit dog biscuits are very tasty! Anyway the point is, are we surprised, I think not!

SUNDAY 13TH JANUARY 2013

It comes to something when you have to take action to ensure work is completed to avoid accidents and injuries. In a Dorset town circles painted in white with an arrow pointing to potholes have been accompanied by the words "fix me". More than 10 of the markings are believed to have been added to Shore Road and other parts of Swanage within the last week.

I have to believe that an individual or individuals have become so incensed with the no-action council that they have had to take such action as a last resort. However Dorset County Council said such actions were illegal and the potholes had already been identified for repair.

Identifying is one thing, doing is another! Wait for a car, motorcycle or bicycle to have an incident and then get them filled. The Council are more interested in who did the dirty deed and have confirmed anyone caught doing it could be prosecuted. Well, that is alright then?

MONDAY 14TH JANUARY 2013

So the Banks and FSA are set to put deadline on PPI claims. Thank goodness for that! I, for one, am sick to the back teeth with PPI phone calls at home, at work and on my mobile. I am inundated with texts confirming I can claim hundreds if not thousands of pounds as I have been miss sold an insurance policy with PPI. When I inform the callers I have never had a PPI they have tried to convince me that I have and should make a claim through them. They can become quite nasty when I refuse.

They seem to be an apathetic bunch that preys on the general public to make a schilling or two. Surely there cannot be anyone left in the UK who is eligible to make a claim? The possible time scale could be set for next summer. What is wrong with today?

TUESDAY 15TH JANUARY 2013

The Government has just announced a pay cut for the finest. The ones we put in the front line when there is a civil disturbance, violent robbery and even a domestic dispute. They get spat at, knifed and shot at so it is gratifying to know they receive the support from the coalition! NOT!

I am talking about the thin blue line, the bobbies, the peelers who have served this country well for decades. The Government has announced they will be reducing a policeman's pay by £4000 pa. What sort of reward is that? Some Government officials and civil servants are completely in the dark about the real world and are happy in their cosy little work environment they have totally switched off.

They are so far up their arses they can poke their heads out of their nostrils their hands out of their ears and stick two fingers up to the rest of us! The very people who deserve the best working conditions and rewards are the police! No discussion!

WEDNESDAY 16TH JANUARY 2013

Oh dear, I have an apology to make. Yesterday I lambasted the Government and civil servants for cutting Police pay by up to £4000 pa. Forgive me as I did not have all the facts at the time and I have made a grave error of judgment. How silly of me.

Today it has been announced that the MP's are suggesting that they are grossly underpaid and need a pay rise. Some MPs said they were underpaid on £65,738 a year. Oh dear how on earth do they survive? Maybe you now understand why they need to fiddle their expenses!

On average, MP's said they deserved salaries of £86,250 — a 32 per cent rise. One in five MP's thought they deserved at least £95,000 a year. More than a third also thought they should keep generous final salary pensions. So now I fully understand that police pay needs to be cut to make a pot of money for the MP's pay increase. Again, how silly of me not to understand the fiscal arguments involved.

THURSDAY 17TH JANUARY 2013

It is just another example of one rule for one and another law for another. Now I am the first to complain if individuals flout the law and try to undermine the lawful system. Rules and regulations are there to support all and if they are wrong then campaign to get them changed and I am at the top of the pile for doing just that!

A couple who built a £500,000 house disguised as a barn on green belt land have been ordered to pull it down. Mr Beesley bought 22 acres) of open green belt land at Northaw in 1999, and was later granted planning permission for a hay barn. Alan and Sarah Beesley won permission to build the hay barn but fitted it out as a home and moved in.

Four years later they applied for permission to use the building as a home but this was denied, sparking a long-running legal battle. Now the Planning Inspectorate has ruled the barn should be demolished. Then why is it the case that, "Travellers" can purchase green belt land, rip it up and lay down concrete and gravel to put their caravans on and erect unsightly sheds and outhouses. This is yet another case of hitting a soft target and leaving the real culprits alone to create wanton damage around them. As I have said many times council officials are not bulldogs they are poodles with no balls!

FRIDAY 18TH JANUARY 2013

I have always thought it strange why we collect things. I mean, why do we do it in the first place? Whether it is cigarette cards, stamps, coins, train numbers or even newspapers, we all like to do our bit in the land of bizarre and weird. I have to admit I include myself in this category after all fancy shaped beer bottles and beer mats have always had a fascination, and in some ways still do.

But Smurf memorabilia you have to be kidding me? Why! A lady in Scotland started collecting when she was six years old when she bought a figurine of a Grouchy Smurf holding an umbrella. Her collection now includes 1,200 stickers and books, 1,370 figurines and 117 stationary products and has cost an estimate £20,000. To grow her collection even further she has requested Smurf gifts for birthdays and Christmas. She says "The amount of things you can buy still amazes me — there's still so much that I don't have but at the moment I'd like to focus on the figurines, I think they're the most interesting. Wow I never looked at it this way, an interesting Smurf! Well I am off to the pub to meet Smurfette to catch up on the latest gossip!

SATURDAY 19TH JANUARY 2013

What have bird droppings and music composition have in common? You may well be quite surprised especially if you are a music fan, as an artist, composer and birds have joined forces to produce a piece of music. Artist Kerry Morrison laid manuscript sheets on the ground in Liverpool parks and let birds deposit their droppings. The positions of the droppings represented different musical notes

Composer Jon Hering then transformed the results into a full musical score, and will be played at a premiere. After listening to a very small piece of the composition I have to admit it is very strange with a few bum notes! It reminds me of birds sitting in trees in a park having a poo onto a piece of paper laid on the ground. I am wondering if my two dogs have any musical talent, as they are guaranteed to make a deposit!!

SUNDAY 20TH JANUARY 2013

A new employment opportunity has arisen for those seeking new employment and also for anyone who fancies a change. It is all about the niche in the market place, being adaptable and working on those entrepreneurial skills. You do not need many tools either, just cotton wool and cotton buds. What is it, I hear you say? Pick out your favourite place on the pavement of your choice, put your sign up, and wait for your customers to queue up.

On the streets of Mumbai in India just like the shoe shiners there are ear cleaners. Yes, ear cleaners, just turn up and get your ears cleaned by the gentlemen with his cotton buds and cotton balls. He will also clean them while you wait. Now that is what I call a good service. Can you hear me? I SAID CAN YOU HEAR ME? I suppose my idea has fallen on deaf ears!!

MONDAY 21ST JANUARY 2013

It is so sad to see boarded up public houses and chinese restaurants in the village high street where the centre of the community used to stand. The village pub was the icon of our villages along with the village green. The demise of our british public houses has been caused by three things. The greedy councils with their extortionate business taxes, the government with their illogical taxes on wines and spirits and thirdly the stupid decision allowing supermarkets to sell alcohol at discount prices.

If it were not for these three ingredients we would have a thriving pub trade where members of the community can meet up talk bollocks, put the world to rights, have a good laugh and go back home and have Saturday night sex, sometimes with their partners. This has got to change as it is one more thing eroding away at the british way of life.

The government does not seem to care and you have to ask the question why? Is there maybe an influence from europe as we get bombarded with the so called european way of life. Now that is a prime example seeing how they are all bankrupt and migrating to the British Isles. Remember Croatia could be joining the EU in 2013 with eight more european countries waiting in the wings next year – Be warned!

TUESDAY 22ND JANUARY 2013

At last, a chink of light shines down into the darkened room that is common sense. A growing number of off licences in a residential area of Peterborough could be halted "**IF**" new licensing laws are agreed. The action comes after it was discovered there are 93 alcohol outlets in the small Millfields area. Now forgive me, for one thing how does the council, who licence these establishments suddenly, discover there are 93? Can they not add up or use their abacus anymore? I call it gross mismanagement from the very people who are supposed to be our guardians. So, our guardians who have cocked the process up want new powers to combat future requests. The council toothless bulldogs have made a decision without further ado. They have decided to "recommend that consultation and further research be carried out into the policy." Well that should do it then, and combat violence and anti-social behaviour.

WEDNESDAY 23RD JANUARY 2013

The police in Peterborough have lodged a complaint which, if not handled correctly, could have an impact on us all. It is a major concern. The police concern is at "swimsuit" barber plans. Yes you read it here the police are concerned that ladies wearing skimpy outfits whilst cutting hair may be a distraction for vehicle drivers passing the shop and cause an accident. The swimsuit barbers shop was the brain wave of Miss T Kiszewska a Polish resident in Peterborough who says they are common, and doing great business back in her homeland Poland. The police have not actually received any complaints yet but Councillor John Peach is concerned about what the business would bring to the area. Oh no not people who want their haircut, that is disgusting. The next popular porn movie could be "short back and sides please!" whisper whisper wink wink nudge nudge. Well I am off for a blow wave, catch you later!

THURSDAY 24TH JANUARY 2013

A lesson to be learnt by us all then! Do not use the texting facility on your phone whilst walking. After all it does involve at least three things walking, looking and texting all at the same time. This may be difficult for some of us. A woman in Birmingham was doing these three things together and she managed to walk in to a freezing cold canal in the city centre. CCTV cameras in the Mailbox shopping district of Birmingham recorded the moment Laura Safe walked straight into the canal while composing a text to her boyfriend. Well she certainly made a splash for herself. Quite ironic surname really! Ms Safe was pulled to safety moments later by a passer-by, with her health if not her pride fully intact.

FRIDAY 25TH JANUARY 2013

Common sense has prevailed again! Gary the goat is a fee man, err free goat! Gary has been cleared by an Australian court of destroying a flower bed outside a Sydney museum. The flower-eating goat's graze with the law ended after a judge ruled neither he nor his owner could be found guilty of vandalism of the incident in August. Police at the time levelled a fine of AUS$440 (£292) against owner Jim Dezarnaul, a comedian known as Jimbo Bazoobi. But man and goat got their day in court, with Gary arriving resplendent in a colourful hat on Wednesday. The brown-and-white goat did not testify, but he had his own lawyer. Magistrate Carolyn Barkell said the accused had been eating the flowers when police arrived, but said there was no evidence Gary was there with the intention of vandalising vegetation. The goat's lawyer Paul McGirr said the police had issued the wrong penalty order, because it related to a person and not a goat. Owner Mr Dezarnaul said the case serves as a lesson to overzealous authorities. "Gary's name has been cleared of all this slander," he said. "He was simply eating and I want to thank everyone for coming down here. "Gary the goat taught the cops a valuable lesson today, don't bite off more than you can chew." Here here, well done Gary can't wait for the book to be published!

SATURDAY 26TH JANUARY 2013

Here we go round the mulberry bush, or is it the carousel, or is it Déjà-vu? The UK Government is to provide £21m in new humanitarian aid for people caught up in the crisis in Syria. International Development Secretary Justine Greening said the aid would "help deliver life-saving winter clothing, food and medicine". He also said it would not be enough, even though the UK has now provided £89.5m in aid for Syria. Now I agree it is very sad when innocent victims get caught up in conflicts and there are thousands happening around the globe. So are we to food all of the other conflicts as well then? I for one would like to be asked and consulted if the British government intends to give away millions of our money to a cause which will probably draw us into yet another conflict where we get involved and OUR people die. The conflict is not of our making and nothing to do with us. The Syrians will turn on us just like Libya and Egypt. They are not our friends and it is nothing to do with us. Look after our own and spend £89.5m on schools, reduce the amount of VAT and income tax we pay or even look after elderly. Now that would be a major change for our government. Mr Cameron and Justine Greening in particular, listen to the voices of discontent.

SUNDAY 27T7H JANUARY 2013

Car parking has always been a sore point with me, after all most of the time it is a case of having to park to go shopping in City centres where you spend money in the retail outlets. I have always seen it as a necessary evil. But should it really be a form of income for the council? Peterborough profits have shot up 45 per cent mainly due to the new ANPR smart cars which roam around the streets catching unsuspecting motorists. Ah, I hear you cry they should not have been parked illegally in the first place. Correct, and that is where I have dichotomy. I agree, but councils tend to paint double yellow lines everywhere they can, including over dead hedgehogs, to maximise their income.

How much income? Well in 2011/2012 Peterborough's was £2,199.000, a tidy little sum in anyone's language. Peterborough is not the worst of course, in London Kensington and Chelsea recorded an income of £27.5 million. Not bad at all, I wonder where the money was spent. Oh, silly me it may have been sent to Syria of course, I mean why spend wisely in the UK?

MONDAY 28TH JANUARY 2013

If it is important enough then make a stand on it that has always been my philosophy. In East Sussex the town council is upsetting its residents by switching off the street lights at 10 pm with a view to cost savings. Now I have always thought that the purpose of street lights was to light up the area in the dark. This gives some protection to the local residents against muggers, rapists and thugs.

Another point of interest is that the local community are the very people who pay the council tax, so they have a right to have a say in where their money is spent. The locals have started a campaign, spearheaded by local radio station Seafordsurf Radio fighting for the locals to stay safe.

There is also going to be a government e-petition raised so watch this space for details. This issue is not going to go away!

TUESDAY 29TH JANUARY 2013

Just like the Northern Island dispute this one will never ever be resolved either. Feelings run too deep for any reconciliation to take place. Argentina's foreign minister has turned down a Foreign Office invitation to meet members of the Falkland Islands government in London next week. Hector Timerman rejected the offer, saying: "The international community does not recognise a third party in this dispute." Well that is point one, Argentina does not recognise the very people who live and inhabit the Falklands Islands. Excuse me, but the people who live on this rocky outlet have made their feelings very clear and I will spell it out in big words for Hector Timerman **THE FALKLAND ISLANDERS DO NOT WHAT ANYTHING TO DO WITH ARGENTINA NOW P**S OFF.**

A referendum on the islands' political status is to be held in March. Argentina will not take any note of the outcome of course they will still continue to harass the population and commit unlawful and intimidating acts. Last year marked 30 years since the Falklands War - when the islands were unlawfully occupied by Argentine forces for 74 days.

WEDNESDAY 30TH JANUARY 2013

Now when I came across this article my initial reaction was one of surprise and in some ways amusement. I am sure we would all like that extra day off at the weekend, after all two days is never enough. The Gambia has shortened the work week, making Friday a day of rest. Public sector workers will now clock in at 8 am and clock out at 6 pm, Monday to Thursday. They'll still do a 40-hour week but have the luxury of Friday off.

President Jammeh wants the extra rest day to "allow Gambians to devote more time to prayers, social activities and agriculture". A fantastic concept indeed! The trouble is the majority of us would use this extra day to go shopping for items we do not really need, to put in the backs of our cupboards to be chucked two years after the use by date. I do however believe President Jammeh is on the right track. Saturday morning is for shopping (if we have to) Saturday afternoon for football and Sunday for the family. Close all supermarkets on Sundays and get to know the family again.

THURSDAY 31ST JANUARY 2013

Oh dear oh dear I have always thought shopping to be a dangerous business that may be the reason I dislike "unnecessary" shopping. You know what I mean, when you go into your local shop or supermarket for one item and then come out with a trolley load of items you do not really need, after you have succumbed to the power of advertising.

An 83-year-old has been banned from her local Tesco store after being accused of bullying staff and deliberately ramming them with her trolley when she became frustrated with slow service. Now that I can relate to, not that I condone violence or intimidation in any form.

Christine Crow was also told she was no longer welcome for being rude and abusive to employees at the supermarket on the Shirley and Hall Green border in Birmingham. The pensioner denied the accusations and is now demanding an apology. She has complained about being snubbed by staff and humiliated.

But Tesco is standing by its decision with one worker, who asked not to be named, claiming a colleague refused to go on the shop floor while the pensioner was there. Oh dear it gets worse. The pensioner was ushered from the premises by two managers and a security guard 'It's a trumped-up charge,' protested Christine 'Bullying? You must be joking. 'Admittedly, the trolleys can have a mind of their own. You bump into someone else's and apologise, but 'ramming' suggests a deliberate act.' The drama unfolded at the deli counter when she spoke out over slow service. She admits being 'sharp'. 'I may have said, "Is there no one serving?". Oh sharp words indeed! Tesco have been unable to provide video camera evidence of the alleged offence. So you all be careful out there and make sure your wobbly wheeled trolleys go in the correct direction! Happy customer shopping experience!

FRIDAY 1ST FEBRUARY 2013

Well believe it or not today is World Hijab Day and it calls upon non-Muslim women to try out life under the traditional head scarf. Can it lead to more religious tolerance and understanding? I am not too sure about that but I have learnt that a Muslim scarf is not just a scarf. Coming in up to seven different varieties it seems to be a statement made by the wearer.

For many people, the hijab is a symbol of oppression and divisiveness. It's a visible target that often bears the brunt of a larger debate about Islam in the West. World Hijab Day is designed to counteract these controversies. It encourages non-Muslim women (or even Muslim women who do not ordinarily wear one) to don the hijab and experience what it's like to do so, as part of a bid to foster better understanding. I am all for it but at the end of the day it is a scarf! I believe tomorrow will be "wearing a cross for a day" to gain an understanding of Christianity, the following day may be "Hari Krishna day", when we can roam the streets banging drums and jangling bells in our loin clothes. Any other ideas please let me know.

SATURDAY 2ND FEBRUARY 2013

Now all of us, or certainly most of us are being hit hard by the austerity measures which have been introduced by this coalition government. I am not going to say it was not needed after the fiasco of the labour government however I would like to believe we are all in it together and we all do our bit for our country. However there always anomalies and exceptions to the rule, but there is always one constant in this equation, councilors. City Councilors in Peterborough are to vote on their pay increase which could be up to 12 pc. This is when the authority considers cutting services to fill a £12 m black hole. This is really pulling together but I do lose sleep at night wondering how our Councilors are going to cope!

SUNDAY 3RD FEBRUARY 2013

Always a sad affair when a long term member of the community falls from grace, especially when they have served well for many years. And who would have predicted that a speeding fine which resulted in three penalty points was the cause of the demise of a long career. It is alleged that between 12 March and 21 May 2003, the ex wife of MP Chris Huhne Ms Pryce, falsely informed police that she was the driver of the car so he could avoid prosecution. She was awarded three penalty points on her driving licence. It subsequently turned out that he was the driver of the vehicle not her. Even though it has been over a decade he has been found out and now resigned his seat as an MP. This is just another example of an individual in authority who believe they are above the law and better than the rest of us. He has resigned and should now be punished for lying in court, committing perjury and above all letting his constituency down.

Update 1: How the mighty fall. Both Chris Huhne and Ms Pryce have both been jailed for their deceit and lying in the witness box. All because of three penalty points and a marriage breakup! Was it really worth it?

MONDAY 4TH FEBRUARY 2013

Oh dear oh dear apparently the Romanian Foreign Minister Titus Corlatean is not happy with the tone of the debate surrounding Romanian and Bulgarian immigration to the UK. Transitional controls on freedom of movement, imposed when the two countries joined the EU in 2007, expire at the end of 2013 - and there is pressure on the government to prevent a significant wave of migrants arriving. Well let's just hope someone, somewhere with the corridors of power actually listen to the people making these claims. We all know that when the restrictions are lifted there will an influx of migrants seeking work like a tidal wave when a damn bursts. There are already an estimated three million Romanians working abroad within the EU, and most observers in Bucharest argue that the vast majority of people who want to leave have already gone. I somehow doubt if that is remotely true otherwise there would not be these rumblings coming out of Romania. British think-tank which campaigns for tighter immigration controls, Migration Watch, has estimated that about 50,000 people from Romania and Bulgaria will come to the UK every year until 2019, with significant consequences for housing and jobs. The British government is always wishy washy on these important issues, as they do not like to upset anyone but now is the time to speak up and say **"NO MORE IMMIGRATION THE COUNTRY IS FULL!"**

TUESDAY 5TH FEBRUARY 2013

Well St Valentine's Day is not that far away now so panic stations, what to do for your loved one? A box of chocolates a bunch of flowers a surprise holiday or a lock? Apparently hundreds of couples are leaving 'love locks' across London ahead of Valentine's Day, attaching them to fences around the capitol. Hundreds of padlocks bearing the names of lovers have appeared across bridges in London. In a custom that is thought to have originated in Hungary in the 1980s, couples leave the locks in a place that is important to them and then throw the key in the water as a symbol of their hearts locking together in eternal love. Occasionally, lovers leave the key in the lock until they can return to their cherished location.

More than 100 have been secured to the grids on Tower Bridge while others have been left along the Embankment. Other locks have appeared in less romantic places, such as on a fence guarding a derelict piece of land near Shoreditch train station. Locks have even appeared in countries and cities around the world from China to Paris. In Rome the number of locks left on the Ponte Milvio Bridge on the river Tiber was so large last year that authorities stepped in after claiming they were harming the structure.

Officials in London said that in some cases they have removed the locks to stop the trend catching on. Kill joys, it is better than a baying mob pelting authorities for the hell of it. Loving symbols like this should be encouraged. How about locking all the MP's in the houses of parliament and insist they actually make a decision together and sort out the mess this country is in. Now I am in fantasy land, there goes a pink valentine pig flying overhead!

WEDNESDAY 6TH FEBRUARY 2013

Now I have a great deal of time for Prince Charles and I believe he actually cares a great deal about this country and the world in which we all live. I am also convinced although he does speak out on a number of issues I believe he is sometimes gagged by the authorities as he gets too near the truth. This time he has waded into battle with a council over the closure of historic kipper smokehouse that survived Blitz. It is in fact Britain's oldest working fish smokehouse and has been shut down after a single resident complained about the smell.

It had survived for more than 130 years and was bombed in the Blitz but Walter Purkis and Sons was told to close by Haringey council following a complaint from a resident in a nearby flat block in Crouch End, North London. The Purkis family was informed last month the smokehouse was in breach of the Environmental Protection Act 1990 and the Clean Air Act 1993.

Absolutely pathetic and the council members who supported this absurd decision should all resign from their positions within the council chamber. The Prince of Wales, a strong supporter of traditional and organic foods, has stepped in to help the owner of the business, whose family has been in the fish business for generations. Last week a female member of the Prince's staff came to see the Purkis family and asked for details about what had happened. It was explained that the smokehouse won a reprieve and was once again allowed to produce its kippers, smoked salmon and mackerel. However the family were worried the reversal of the ban may only be temporary. Sanity at last and considering the smokehouse has been there for over 130 years I would say to the resident who complained, shut up, get a life and move so far away the only thing you can smell is your deodorant!

THURSDAY 7TH FEBRUARY 2013

One thing that grinds my gears is people steeling items and property from others who have saved their money and bought their items legally. Steeling is against the law and when caught these criminals must be punished when proved guilty. It amused me somewhat when I read an article where a man attempted to siphon petrol from a motor home parked on a Seattle Street However he got much more than he bargained for. Police arrived at the scene to find an ill man curled up next to a motor home when trying to steal the petrol and had plugged his hose into the motor home's sewage tank by mistake. The owner of the vehicle declined to press charges, saying that it was the best laugh he'd ever had. Personally speaking it is just deserts!

FRIDAY 8TH FEBRUARY 2013

Ever wondered what it would be like to win the lottery? Like me you probably dream occasionally how you would spend a few thousand pound or even the odd million.
As we would be Californian Bill Helko was thrilled when he had the winning numbers in the local lottery, the first prize being $412,000.
He straight away went and ordered a Porsche, booked a family holiday in Hawaii and had a champagne dinner with his wife and friends at an expensive Hollywood restaurant.
When he went to pick up the winnings he found that 9,097 others had also won first prize and his share of the jackpot was $45. So the moral of the story, before quitting your job and spending some of the winnings wait until it is in your bank account and has been cleared or you could be in an embarrassing fiscal position.

SATURDAY 9TH FEBRUARY 2013

Be careful do not fall for the old scams and there are many of them. Fraudsters and con artists seem to be one step ahead all the time in trying to obtain you're hard earned cash. Some criminals get caught and punished of course but there are some who do not get caught and in fact are very clever at what they do.

Australian Police have been unable to recommend a prosecution for the following scam:
A company takes out a newspaper advertisement claiming to be able to supply imported hard core pornographic videos. As their prices seem reasonable, people place orders and make payments via cheque.
After several weeks, the company writes back explaining that under the present law they are unable to supply the materials and do not wish to be prosecuted. So they return their customers' money in the form of a company cheque. However, due to the name of the company, few people will present these cheques to their banks. The name of the company: **"The Anal Sex and Fetish Perversion Company."** You have been warned!

SUNDAY 10TH FEBRUARY 2013

Vehicle mechanics are well known for bearing the brunt of jokes and humorous stories but it was interesting to read this article recently. An auto mechanic received a repair order that read: "Check for clunking sound when going around corners." Taking the car out for a test drive, he made a right turn, and a moment later he heard a 'clunk'. He then made a left turn and again heard a 'clunk'. Back at the shop he opened the car's trunk, and soon discovered the problem. Promptly he returned the repair order to the service manager with the notation, "Removed bowling ball from trunk". Moral of the story, "Always check that your balls are in the right place and secured appropriately"

MONDAY 11TH FEBRUARY 2013

Recently there has been a spate of attempted theft of cash machines located in the walls of shops and supermarkets. Indeed it seems all you need is a strong vehicle, a good chain and some guts to pull off the heist. Recently two men tried to pull the front off a cash machine by running a chain from the machine to the bumper of their pickup truck. Instead of pulling the front panel off the machine, though, they pulled the bumper off their truck. Scared, they left the scene and drove home. With the chain still attached to the machine. With their bumper still attached to the chain. With their vehicle's license plate still attached to the bumper. You have to feel for these villains but hey, don't be fooled they are scumbags who will rob you of your personal belongings without a second glance. They are stupid and deserve to get caught. The vehicle should also be impounded, crushed into a small block of mangled metal, dumped and the villains made to pay for the disposal.

TUESDAY 12TH FEBRUARY 2013

We certainly live in a disposable world, more so than at any time and it seems to be getting worse. As you visit your local refuge recycling centre (Local dump to you and me) there are huge skips filled with every item you can think of, besides the usual kitchen waste. There are beds, furniture, kitchens not to mention televisions and DVDs. Everything seems to be disposable including the odd penis here and there. What? Oh yes the very last standing bastion of male supremacy has bit the dust. Apparently, and scientists have spent many hours watching and learning, Sea slug's have disposable penis. A sea slug is able to detach, re-grow and then re-use its penis has surprised Japanese scientists. Who have observed the bizarre mating behaviour in a species called Chromodoris reticulata, which is found in the Pacific Ocean? They believe this is the first creature known that can repeatedly copulate with what they describe as a "disposable penis". Almost all of these creatures, which are also known as nudibranchs, are thought to be "simultaneous hermaphrodites". This means they have both male and female sexual organs and can use them both at the same time.

However, the researchers were surprised to discover that just 24-hours later, the sea slugs had regenerated their male organs and were able to mate again. Closer examination of the animals' anatomy revealed that the sea slugs had a large part of their penis coiled up in a spiral inside their bodies, which they would then use to replenish their missing part.

The scientists also noted that the penis was also equipped with spines. At most, the animals were able to copulate three times in succession, with each bout separated by about 24 hours. Not too sure about it myself but as I say we live in a disposable world. 'Nuff said!!

WEDNESDAY 13TH FEBRUARY 2013

Are you a "Down'ard" or an "Up'ard?" That is a key question if you were born or reside in the Derbyshire town of Ashbourne. Every year two teams battle it out over two days to score goals in goalposts which are three miles apart. The Royal Shrovetide Football game draws crowds in their thousands lining the streets to watch the game which is played over two days Shrove Tuesday and ends on Ash Wednesday. The game, which dates back to the Middle Ages, has been described as a disorganised rugby scrum. It truly is a unique game and a tradition the town's folk are very proud of - whichever side of the fence - or river - they were born.

The 2013 game began when local builder John Tompkinson "turned up" the ball at 14:00 GMT on Shrove Tuesday. Dave Spencer was said to have been the first goaler of the day at Sturston - shortly after 21:00 GMT. Shops have boarded up their windows and businesses have closed early for the event.

Hundreds of players for each side battled in the streets on Tuesday to get the hand-painted cork-filled ball to goals three miles apart. There are rules of course players must keep out of churchyards, cemeteries and memorial gardens, transporting the ball in cars and killing your opponents are also forbidden Each team goals by banging the ball three times on a single post at either Clifton or Sturston and each team goals at their own end of the town with leading players drawing lots for who will be allowed to goal. Up to four games are played over two days with unconfirmed reports of several injuries during the first day of the game. Goals are mill wheels set in huge stone plinths on the banks of the Henmore Brook at the sites of two former mills. To score, a player must stand in the Henmore and tap the ball three times against the wheel. Scoring means you will be carried back into the town by your team shoulder high and cheered by hundreds of spectators.

Now I have the dubious pleasure in admitting I was an "Up'ard" back in the seventies and I actually touched the ball during a game. I must admit it is a frightening experience as the crowd has difficulty in moving, due to the numbers and you may be stationery for half an hour before the ball may break free and off you go again. Ah, good old British traditions, just love 'em!

THURSDAY 14TH FEBRUARY 2013

A couple were going on holiday but his wife was on a business trip so he went to the destination first and his wife arranged to meet him the next day. When he arrived at the hotel, he decided to send his wife a quick email. Unfortunately, when typing her e-mail address he mistyped a letter and his note was directed instead to an elderly preacher's wife whose husband had passed away only the day before. When the grieving widow checked her email, she took one look at the monitor, let out a piercing scream, and fell to the floor in a dead faint. At the sound, her family rushed into the room and saw this note on the screen:

Dearest Wife just got checked in. Everything prepared for your arrival tomorrow. P.S. Sure is hot down here.

FRIDAY 15TH FEBRUARY 2013

We spend more on benefits in this country than we do on the NHS so it is not surprising that the government is always reviewing the system. However even David Cameron may not have thought of this new benefit give away. It is the Jihad Seeker's Allowance. Anjem Choudary the scrounging hate preacher has told fanatics to scrounge and copy him by going on benefits — urging: "Claim your Jihad Seeker's Allowance." He cruelly ridicules non-Muslims who held down 9-to-5 jobs all their lives and said sponging off them made plotting holy war easier and predicted a tsunami" of Islamic immigrants would sweep Europe. Strange, I thought that had already happened! Father-of-four Choudary, who has praised terrorist outrages, pockets more than £25,000 a year in benefits — £8,000 more than the take-home pay of some soldiers fighting the Taliban in Afghanistan. Figures obtained by The Sun in 2010 showed the extremist cleric received £15,600 a year in housing benefit to keep him in a £320,000 house in Leytonstone, East London. He also got £1,820 council tax allowance, £5,200 income support and £3,120 child benefits — equivalent to a taxed salary of £32,500. Well who is the stupid party in this one then? It is you and me the ordinary working people of this land who allow this to happen. You and I are working so we can give this evil person thousands and keep him in a living style we can only dream of. He is an evil and ungodly person who will go to hell, and that is where we should tell him to go.

SATURDAY 16TH FEBRUARY 2013

The law forbidding smoking in public places has its followers and those who do not agree with it. Each of us has a personal view and in a democracy the majority opinion may be the one which should be followed. However there are still places where the law is quite blatantly flouted. However we all have a choice whether to go inside these premises or not and that is quite right! On a recent visit to London we visited Stockwell which is not too far from Clapham common where we were on a walking trip. We decided to stop at a local hostelry for refreshment and a rest. Now this day and age with public houses closing at hundreds a week you do not find a pub on every street corner like it used to be. We did however come across The Duke of Cambridge which I can only describe as having an exterior like a concrete jungle. It looked cold and unwelcoming and noticing the external benches fixed to the walls with heavy chains should have set the alarm bells ringing. Entering the establishment we were greeted with total darkness and unable to go more than three yards as there was a table blocking the way. There was a way around the left hand side but that was blocked by three burley gentlemen, one of which began to frisk me, which took me by surprise a little bit. Anyway the point is the establishment was thick with rancid smoke you could not breathe in. We were shepherded to the bar and ordered our drinks which turned out to be slightly on the watered down side. Maybe one for trip advisor!!!

SUNDAY 17TH FEBRUARY 2013

Planning a visit to your local GP is always a hassle and certainly a pain in the ass, if that is a symptom of your medical condition of course! As previously blogged the first step is getting passed the receptionist who always knows better than you the reason why you do not need to visit your GP. If you do eventually get an appointment for three weeks time then the real battle begins. You try to explain your symptoms to the doctor when they do not really understand you and conversely you cannot understand them, as they do not speak the mother tongue fluently. Absolutely bonkers! There was a time when your local GP was YOUR local GP and they knew and understood your body better than you did, but those days are long gone. So called professional doctors from every corner of the planet have been practicing here for years and getting away with it and in return our health has suffered as a result. So now, the government has finally agreed that foreign doctors wanting to treat NHS patients in England will have to prove they have the necessary English skills. Wow, that must have been a difficult decision to make! From April 2013 there will be a legal duty to ensure a doctor's English is up to scratch before they are employed and they will have to prove they can speak a "necessary level of English" before they are allowed to treat patients in hospitals or in GP surgeries. Well whoopee doo! Let's hope it is more of a test than being able to write their names on a prescription!

MONDAY 18TH FEBRUARY 2013

Thinking of moving house in the near future? If so make sure you are in the correct one before spending out giving it a makeover. A businessman in China purchased a flat only to find out, after spending out £20,000 he was in the wrong one. An expensive lesson indeed, but how could that happen? Mr Gui Lizhong was sold flat 4-2 in a new development in Chongqing, China before the numbers were on the doors. He only realised he had mistakenly decorated 4-1 when Mr Long Nengyun turned up and produced paperwork showing he was the owner. Apparently he had purchased flat 4-2 in 2011. The mistake may have arisen after a saleswoman twice took Mr Lizhong to view the apartment. "I viewed the house twice before I signed the contract," Gui said. "The property agent showed me this particular unit." The saleswoman denied this version of events and insisted she had shown him the right property. Any hope the unfortunate man could keep his new apartment were dashed after Mr Long refused to exchange the homes.

TUESDAY 19TH FEBRUARY 2013

Do you or have you travelled on the London underground? It can sometimes be a pitiful experience with delays and engineering works. Loud speakers blare out information which is inaudible and of little assistance for you when planning your route. So it is gratifying to learn there is a little ray of sunshine in the murky depths. A worker on the Victoria line making passengers smile with his jovial announcement to commuters in a Caribbean accent and it has become an instant hit. The staff member in charge of giving information to the passengers decided he'd had enough of the boring monotone normally associated with London's subway network, so made his own special announcement – complete with Caribbean slang. *'This train is for all de Brixton crew. Service update, everyting irie, everyting cris. Chill out, kick back, no need let anybody cramp your style,'* the guard says in a relaxed tone. *'Rastaman driver, take these beautiful people to their destination.'* He is brilliant and let's hope other announcers take the hint and work on their delivery. One word of caution! What will be the odds on this happy chappie being disciplined by his superiors for not sticking to the rules of the underground?

WEDNESDAY 20TH FEBRUARY 2013

Coincidentally after the news that foreign doctors coming into the UK to practice will need to take an English test it appears they may not be the only ones who have difficulty in reading and writing in English. Bungling council workers have been left embarrassed after misspelling the word Welsh on a road sign in Shropshire. It was put by the roadside to advise drivers that the town's Grade II listed Welsh Bridge was closed on Sunday for roadworks. The bridge crosses the River Severn and connects the Frankwell area of Shrewsbury with the town centre. Baffled drivers could be seen double-taking as they approached the sign which instead read 'Whelsh Bridge Closed'. This is just another example of a "couldn't care less" attitude of the people responsible for undertaking the task correctly. The individuals should be ashamed of themselves and perhaps they need a refresher course in the mother tongue or is it a case of employing foreigners who do not have a clue about this country? The jury is out on that one I think!

THURSDAY 21ST FEBRUARY 2013

I have often blogged there may be a number of slime balls in government and sitting in council chambers and now it appears it is prevalent in Somerset. The origin of a mysterious 'slime' substance that has appeared at a nature reserve in Somerset has baffled experts. "This past week we've been finding piles of this translucent jelly dotted around the reserve," Steve Hughes, the RSPB site manager at Ham Wall, said. No-one has definitively stated what the substance is but that hasn't stopped many of them guessing what it could be. One popular theory is that it is a form of cyan bacteria called Nostoc but others have suggested it could be the regurgitated innards of amphibians such as frogs and toads and of their spawn. There you go then I was correct in my assumption the slime was a government or council official!

FRIDAY 22ND FEBRUARY 2013

As regular readers of this blog are aware I have been having problems with my laptop. Of course, the glass of red wine spilt over the keyboard did not help, but not one but two replacement computers encountered critical errors and crashed. The unfortunate incident happened on the 6th December 2012 and I am still awaiting a suitable and working replacement from the insurance company. Anyway, I digress. The replacement laptops which were the same make and model had a very sensitive mouse pad and even hovering over it made weird things happen on screen. In fact it had a mind of its own and deleted and moved words and images at a whim. Of course I thought it was me! But apparently not! On a visit to the physiotherapist for a neck injury it was somehow gratifying to see his laptop with a piece of cardboard taped across the mouse pad to render it inoperative. It made my day knowing I was not the only one in the universe being a tecky nerd!

SATURDAY 23RD FEBRUARY 2013

Can world peace ever be established? Will the world be united? Is there anything the powers have in common? Well, the answer may be yes, and it could all be down to SpongeBob squarepants. Russian soldiers have turned to TV cartoon SpongeBob SquarePants in a bid to keep their spirits high while marching to the beat. Despite temperatures dropping well below zero during the country's winter months, Russia's army personnel refuse to let the weather get them down. They have surprisingly taken a shine to the lovable bright yellow sponge, gleefully chanting his name while marching in unison. The SpongeBob theme song is one of the most popular marching songs with both ground infantry troops and navy sailors, according to englishrussia.com. The real army captains got used to training their voices to match the SpongeBob's captain's voice when he asks "Are you ready children???". So there you have it, SpongeBob squarepants is the saviour of the world. Sounds about right to me! After all we have tried everything else, and it is better than shooting each other.

SUNDAY 24THTH FEBRUARY 2013

Pussy has always been a favourite of mine and I am sure fifty percent of the world would agree with me but opening a cafe for pussy I am not too sure. The UK's first-ever cat café is coming to London in the next couple of months after members of the public donated over £100,000 to make one cat lover's dream a reality.

What?

Entrepreneur Lauren Pears has already started looking at prospective sites in the Old Street area of London and is aiming to have the café up and running by May 2013 The 30-year-old claims she has already found the 10 to 15 cats which will staff the café, with the animals coming from the Mayhew Animal Home in Kensal Green, north-west London. Customers will be able to stroke the 10-15 cats during their time in the cafe

Oh come on stroking pussy whilst having a drink?

Ms Pears, who was inspired by the popular cat cafes in Japan, said she spotted a gap in the market with large numbers of British city dwellers unable to have pets of their own due to living in rented accommodation, small flats or financial constraints. The café will provide a place where cat lovers can stroke the roaming felines while drinking their coffee. 'We tried to figure out a solution where the cats don't get too stressed out which is why we've introduced the cover charge,' Ms Pears told the Independent.

Hold on why should an excited pussy get a cover charge?

The cafe is sure to attract cat lovers from all over London, "That way, people can stay as long as they like without feeling like they're against the clock which works for the cats because it takes cats a little time to get used to people."

This is just so unreal pussy should not be enjoyed against the clock, it takes time and patience.

She added: "We're going to have a volunteer programme so people who can't afford the cover charge can actually come in overnight and look after the cats."

Ah an overnight pussy!

Cat cafes are popular in Japan and last year Vienna also opened a similar type of eatery.

Ah ha a pussy eatery!

Now that is what I call a first class restaurant. Thank you Lord!

MONDAY 25TH FEBRUARY 2013

Well they say we are all getting bigger so more and more services are being provided for the "oversized", and sport is no exception. Supersize seats for super-fat football fans in Brazil are being provided for the supersize footie fan. Thought sport was supposed to encourage a healthy attitude, but perhaps not. Supersize seats have been constructed to hold obese football fans during next year's World Cup in Rio for the super fatties and the reinforced seats will be able to hold fans that weigh up to 40 stone. However the double-width seats will cost larger fans twice the standard ticket price at the matches in Fortaleza's Castelao stadium. The 120 seats are blue instead of the standard white and have been installed in the 64,000 capacity venue. Let's hope the floors have been reinforced to cater for all the jumping up and down as the wobblies celebrate their team scoring a goal!

TUESDAY 26TH FEBRUARY 2013

Do you like your work colleagues or do you just tolerate them? It may take some time but there are always opportunities to speak your mind about them or in some cases put pen to paper in a covert way. One such example happened in a retirement message to a colleague in Harrow North West London. As retirement announcements go, it seemed kind and innocuous enough. But a prep school headmaster's wordplay has cost him his job after his departing colleague detected a stronger sentiment between the lines. "It is with mixed feelings that I announce the retirement of Mr. Roger Clark at the end of this term," wrote Mark Dunning, the head of the £13,000-a-year Orley Farm School. **W**e **a**ll **n**ow **k**now **e**very **r**eally great teacher has to finish one day and Mr. Clark will do so at the end of this term." What is wrong with that message you ask, it seems to be heartfelt and to the point. Well Mr. Clark spotted that the first letters of the first six words in the second sentence of his retirement announcement spelled out a rather choice insult So, there we have it, choose what you wish to say about your colleague first and then build the message around it. **T**oday **W**e **A**ll **T**ry!

WEDNESDAY 27TH FEBRUARY 2013

There are flash mobs, and there are flash mobs but I am really not too sure about this one. The FAA is investigating an incident on a flight from Denver to San Diego when an entire plane load of passengers took part in a mid-air flash mob. Video shot on the Frontier flight shows passengers jumping up and down mid-flight to the latest viral dance craze - the Harlem Shake. Suddenly everyone is dancing including one guy dressed as a banana and another person wearing an Abraham Lincoln mask. While the video has gone viral with more than 450,000 views on YouTube, safety experts have voiced concerns that the prank unnecessarily put the entire plane in jeopardy. The flash mob was organised by members of the Colorado College Ultimate Frisbee Team who were on their way to a tournament in San Diego over President's Day weekend. Somehow they managed to convince fellow passengers of all ages to get up and pump their fists to the dance tune by DJ Baauer. So there you have it, although I do not condone flashing in public!

THURSDAY 28TH FEBRUARY 2013

Strange world we live in! Syrian President Bashar al-Assad has accused the British government of bullying and naivety in its approach to the conflict in his country. He said "To be frank, Britain has played a famously unconstructive role in our region on different issues for decades, some say for centuries. Frank? Thought is name was Basher, which I suppose is very apt considering about 70,000 people have been killed in the Syrian uprising that started almost two years ago. Hundreds of thousands of refugees have fled to neighbouring countries. He continued "The problem with this government is that their shallow and immature rhetoric only highlights this tradition of bullying and hegemony." Bullying and hegemony, I do not think so Basher, have a look in your own back yard first beyond the outhouse and dead bodies which surround you and which you are solely responsible for.

FRIDAY 1ST MARCH 2013

Air travel is always an experience mostly I have to say a very dire experience which usually ends up with "Oh never again!", but we do it all over again the next time. I remember one such occasion when I was en route to Israel for a week's walking holiday, stopping at a number of kibbutz. Anyway I digress, I was at the airport, and of course with the troubles in the Middle East there are always enhanced security procedures in place. At the check in the airport employee asked, "Has anyone put anything in your baggage without your knowledge?" To which I replied, "If it was without my knowledge, how would I know?" He smiled knowingly and nodded, "that is why we ask".

SATURDAY 2ND MARCH 2013

Pedestrians are always in danger when walking down the road, I know, as I am walking the dogs in the morning the vehicles speed through the village and just do not care about the poor pedestrians and even "get a sense of enjoyment" as they speed through the puddles splashing anything and anyone who dares to get in their way. Crossing the road can also sometimes be an issue so always use a pedestrian crossing to keep safe. I was on a crossing the other morning and a neighbour was also crossing with me. The light came on to cross and the beeper sounded. She enquired if I knew why the beeper sounded. I explained that it signals blind people when the light is red. Appalled she responded, "What on earth are blind people doing driving?"

SUNDAY 3RD MARCH 2013

Seafordsurf Radio Vanburger's Beef Pie Recipe, great for those furlonging for something different

1 pound ground horse meat
2 cups sweet red peppers, with sauce
1 onion, chopped
1 (4.5 ounce) can sliced mushrooms, drained
1 cup shredded sharp Cheddar cheese
1 recipe pastry for a 9 inch double crust pie

Place peppers, including liquid, into food processor; pulse until peppers are cut into small pieces. Brown horse meat and onions then add peppers, mushrooms, and cheese to meat mixture. Spoon into bottom crust. Cover with top crust, and seal the edges.

Bake at 350 degrees F (175 degrees C) until crust is brown, and pie is heated through.

You can get further cookery tips on www.seafordsurfradio.com although I wonder if he is trying to follow in the footsteps of DJ Wayne's bestselling book "Not so perfect cooking"

MONDAY 4TH MARCH 2013

When you are out walking it can always be a little dangerous especially if you are in the vicinity of a roadway. Dangerous places indeed. On one such occasion we were walking though Peterborough city centre when we heard a loud bang, the sort of noise like a vehicle smashing in to a road sign at thirty miles an hour. Which it was! A vehicle somehow had careered off the road and smashed into a give way sign! The driver, a little flustered, got out of the driver's side and walked around to the passenger side and opened the door. He rummaged around in the glove compartment and took out a spectacle case, removed the spectacles and put them on! Need I go on?

WEDNESDAY 6TH MARCH 2013

Are councillors' dummies?

An Aberdeen woman, Renee Slater, has been charged after a mannequin was entered as a candidate in last year's city council election. She was taken to court over the name Helena Torry being put forward to stand in the May election. She was charged under the Representation of the People Act 1983. Returning officer Crawford Langley had told the court he had taken nomination papers from the accused an hour before the close of nominations. Ms Slater was charged with adding a candidate she knew was in fact a mannequin. The defence argued the charge could only apply to a candidate and not an agent. She has been acquitted of the offence and has told the police that she sought to inject humour into an austere process. As for Helena Torry, the mannequin has been held in storage by Grampian Police and is due to be reunited with Ms Slater at a later date. Ah what a lovely story but I have been under the impression this has happened on more than one occasion and has yet to be detected!

THURSDAY 7TH MARCH 2013

Topless protesters staged demonstrations near mosques and Tunisian embassies across Europe to express support for embattled FEMEN activist Amina Tyler. "We're free, we're naked, it's our right, it's our body, it's our rules, and nobody can use religion, and some other holy things, to abuse women, to oppress them," FEMEN member Alexandra Shevchenko said in Berlin, according to AFP. "And we'll fight against them. And our boobs will be stronger than their stones," she added. Tunisian student Amina Tyler sparked a massive controversy in mid-March by posting topless photos of herself on Facebook, with the slogans "F**k Your Morals" and "My Body Belongs To Me, And Is Not The Source Of Anyone's Honour," painted on her body. Islamist hackers responded with an attack on FEMEN's Tunisian Facebook Fan Page, replacing topless photos with quotes from the Quran. An Islamic preacher even stated that Tyler could be stoned for her act of defiance. In support of Tyler's plight, FEMEN labelled April 4 "International Topless Jihad Day" and organised protests across Europe. "This day will mark the beginning of a new, genuine Arab Spring, after which true freedom, freedom without mullahs and caliphs, will come to Tunisia! Long live the topless jihad against infidels!" Our tits are deadlier than your stones! The group wrote in a statement on its Facebook page. Well there you have it, keep abreast of the times and support FEMEN.

FRIDAY 8TH MARCH 2013

Now this is good news and a victory for common sense. A leading London university has banned an Islamic organisation from holding events on its campus after it told women to sit separately from men and couples at a debate there. Audience members at the public debate at University College London (UCL) were told to enter the chamber through either the men's or women's entrances. Event organisers' iERA (Islamic Education and Research Academy) then asked women to sit at the back, while men and couples were allowed to sit at the front. UCL said today that the Islamic Education and Research Academy were no longer allowed to hold events there. When Professor Krauss realised the audience was being segregated before the debate started, he packed his bag and said he was leaving, only returning when he had been persuaded by staff that they would abandon attempts to sit the audience according to gender. Can I politely remind iERA we have a democracy in this country, the very democracy that you are seeking to destroy. Enough is enough we will not stand for this archaic behaviour anymore from individuals who vow to destroy the very environment we live in. If you do not like our customs then you know you can always return to your motherland, or are you too scared and downtrodden over there?

SATURDAY 9TH MARCH 2013

Government schemes come and go quicker than a fiddlers elbow. Some show improvement but many fall by the wayside for varied reasons but this one takes the proverbial biscuit. Towns have spent just 7% of Mary Portas' £10 million fund to rescue High Streets, and most of it went on a reindeer costing £1000 and Eppa Pig costumes. Oh it gets worse! The retail guru was tasked by the government to help revive town centres with 100 towns receiving a share of £10 million fund to attract shoppers but of 72 councils surveyed, 47 still have the money sitting in their bank whilst others have spent it on Christmas fairs despite being warned not to. Councils are continuing to throw taxpayers' money at the same stale ideas they've been peddling for years. Wyre Forest District Council spent £12,000 on bringing 10 empty shops back into use. But a different council spent £10,900 on Christmas lights, while another authority spent £10,038 on a train station ramp. Meanwhile, Swale Borough Council in Kent spent £164.60 on a snow machine. Absolutely disgusting waste of money especially after it has been made available by a government scheme to rejuvenate the town centres. These money wasting councils should be made to pay the money back and forfeit any other schemes to assist them. Spend the money where councils spend it wisely, not the usual councils who believe they have the right to extract money from the residents and spend it on stupid wasteful schemes and then increase the council tax to pay for them. Use your vote wisely at the next local elections. Do not sit on the council fence!

SUNDAY 10TH MARCH 2013

I was interested to read the headline "Palestinian's born from prisoners smuggled sperm" in the paper today. Apparently sperm from convicted bombers and murderers has been smuggled out of Israeli jails and used to impreg the woman, back in their homeland. One such case Ammar Ziben is serving 32 life sentences in an Israeli prison for his involvement in bomb attacks in Jerusalem in 1997. His wife said "my happiness is not complete without my husband here beside me." Well tough on you, he should have thought about that before he started on his murderous bombing spree killing dozens of innocent people. Not only is he a callous murderer but he is a w****r as well!

MONDAY 11TH MARCH 2013

So we, or more accurately, the billions of Catholics across the globe have a new leader to guide them on the straight and narrow. Congratulations on passing the interview Francis and good luck in your new position. I am sure you will get on fine with all that back slapping and ring kissing. You will not have an easy ride of course, with falling church attendances, abortion issues, contraceptive agreement, gay marriage, female Bishops and of course let's not forget the child abuse and sex abuse problems that the church is riddled with. Many issue for you to focus on. So why is it then that the new pontiff who just happens to come from Argentina is poking his almighty nose in to Falkland's politics? He can have his own thoughts of course but stay out of politics. The Falkland Islands are British, read up on the islands history at bedtime; you may be enlightened to discover Argentina does not have a claim just because they have rewritten history in their own language. The people of the Falklands Islands have voted. Mr. Pontiff you of all people should respect the will of the people!

TUESDAY 12TH MARCH 2013

This is for the idiot who was throwing his weight about and injured some youngsters who were just having fun in the snow. The youngsters were having a snowball fight, as kids do, in the newly fallen snow when one snowball accidentally hit a girl who was passing. The boys apologised for the lay snowball to which the girl replied, "You will be when my boyfriend sorts you out", and with that she called her boyfriend on her mobile phone. Within a few minutes the 25 year old boyfriend arrived in his works van, got out and started having a go at the boys. He hit one on the shoulder, one in the head and a third one in the face breaking his nose and one tooth. Needless to say the police have been informed and he will be, quite rightly, prosecuted for causing bodily harm. Two observations here! One, he was well out of order for losing his temper and striking the boys and two, the girl must be as stupid as to take such an offence over being hit by a wayward snowball. She is a dumb ass and should be put in stocks and snowballs thrown at her. As for him he should firstly apologise to those who he struck, made to do community service, naked in the snow wearing a placard with **"I AM A STUPID BAD TEMPERED GIT WHO STRIKES BOYS"** around his neck and then be sentenced for GBH. Oh and also throw snowballs at his stupid girlfriend!

WEDNESDAY 13TH MARCH 2013

Are school children getting more unruly and aggressive or is it the way society has changed. Is it bad parenting, TV influences or the schools? Or is it all these? A young lady who is an assistant at a Secondary modern school was with her seven year old daughter shopping in the local supermarket. There was a crash, she turned around and behind her were a number of youths from her school. They had deliberately dropped and smashed a bottle of drink. She tried to walk away but was hindered by the youths surrounding her. As she picked items off the shelf they were roughly taken from her hand. They blocked her way being rude and aggressive. The young lady responded in a loud voice but the youths did not take any notice. A member of staff who was pregnant told the boys off but again they took no notice and continued to harass the lady. The member of staff quickly reported the incident to the Manager of the store but he did nothing. A male who was shopping came forward and told the boys to stop their harassment, they took little notice but eventually, being rude and aggressive made their way out of the store. The youths were 13 / 14 year olds and harassing a lady, more than twice their age, and her daughter. This has been reported to the police and the youths parents have argued that the lady was at fault for shouting. The lady has been suspended from her school. This is a disgusting slight in the society in which we live. The parents are in some ways worse than the idiotic youths. The youths are examples of what is wrong with society today. The pregnant worker in the store and the male shopper are examples of what is good in society today. The store manager is an example of a lump of dog poo that was on the pavement but is now on the bottom of your shoe.

THURSDAY 14TH MARCH 2013

If you are going to watch porn on your computer make sure you are not at work and certainly make sure nobody can see your screen. No matter how careful you may be there is never really a good time to watch porn at work, no matter how empty you think the office is. But even when you've checked every meeting room, toilet cubicle and the office kitchen to ensure the coast is clear; it is always a good idea to close the blinds. That is what one lonesome worker in Australia learned when he was caught red handed looking at a graphic X-rated video at his desk - by office employees across the street. Lounging in his swivel chair, the unidentified voyeur continued watching the flick, blissfully unaware that he was giving the building opposite a peep show of its very own. But his alone-time was frustratingly cut short when he noticed the gathering crowd of workers at the window behind him. Despite their applause and calls of encouragement, the white-shirted worker bashfully turned off his computer and vanished into a darker corner of his office where he could no longer be seen. Apparently it is not the first time an employee has exposed their predilection for the adult arts to public scrutiny. In December a high school teacher became an internet sensation after he hooked up his laptop to a projector screen in a lecture hall, apparently unaware of the Pornhub.com account notification email sitting at the top of his inbox. As titters rippled through the auditorium, one enterprising student took a picture of the screen and posted it online, thus compounding the teacher's already widespread humiliation. So there you have it, sound advice for when you get the urge to view a spicy film with your TV dinner!

FRIDAY 15TH MARCH 2013

Coincidentally, after a previous blog about unruly youths harassing an innocent young mother in a supermarket this story is a cut above the rest! A family were left horrified after finding a four-inch blade in a loaf of bread from a Morrison's in-store bakery. Andy Newman from south west London, bought the sliced loaf for a Mother's Day lunch last Sunday. His wife reached into the bag to give three-year-old Madison a slice but luckily spotted the large serrated blade before any harm was done The razor-sharp four-inch blade was found sticking out the loaf of Morrison's bread. Mr Newman said, "My wife took out the first slice and put her hand in and as the next slice fell we found the blade sticking out." Mr Newman promptly returned to Morrison's to complain but said he was shocked when the manager first simply offered to refund his £1.30. He said, "The store manager eventually begrudgingly offered me £30 vouchers but she didn't really want to do that. She was prepared to take the bread off me and give me £1.30 back. I said I think it's was a bit more serious than that." Seems to be a trait with managers in supermarket stores, no balls and no gumption!

SATURDAY 16TH MARCH 2013

Oh Boris Oh Boris, I agree with most you say but your latest Boris, I do not think so! Boris Johnson Mayor of London advocates building airports, power plants and railways on the vast swathes of English countryside. What a buffoon, if he did that there would be nowhere for the illegal immigrants to stay! Mr. Johnson used a speech in Paris to call on the Government to be more "ruthless" in the way it builds on the countryside in the future. Ahead of George Osborne's Budget next week, Mr. Johnson said he "wished we could be French in our approach to infrastructure". Oh do me a favour Boris you are talking out of your backside, the French infrastructure is built upon subsidies handed out by the EU, with the majority of the money coming from Britain! Their infrastructure is built around farming and fisheries, both being archaic. They have not moved with the times and they are far from modern. The babbling mouth went on "And I wished we could imitate the ease and ruthlessness with which the French send high speed trains streaking across the landscape." Oh for goodness sake our landscape looks excellent at the moment thank you very much! Babble again, "And as the light bulbs of Britain flicker, I am lost in admiration for the historic French decision to build enough nuclear reactors to supply 75 per cent of your power needs, and in the next 30 years we in Britain will now try to catch up while French companies raise the capital for even more ambitious investments." So there we have it, Boris advocates churning up this green and pleasant land and cover with tarmac and concrete, we all become French, build nuclear reactors so we can all get fried and build the HST link across the most beautiful countryside in the world and which nobody wants. Oo la la!

SUNDAY 17TH MARCH 2013

Orange help desk:
Ring ring ring ring
"We are very busy at the moment there is a wait of 45 minutes!"
What? Is that why they changed to **HE HE**
Orange Internet help:
"No access at the moment we are striving to improve our service try again later"
A long way to go then!
HE HE HA HA Whatever!

MONDAY 18TH MARCH 2013

It is official! Sitting is a danger to your health, according to officials at a shopping centre in West Midlands! They foresee mortal danger in the most mundane of situations – but health and safety officials have surely outdone themselves with a ban on sitting down. Customers at a shopping centre are no longer allowed to rest their weary legs in case they trip up passers-by. The ruling affects a canopied area that is raised six inches from the main concourse. 'Elf and safety? Ryemarket Shopping Centre in the West Midlands has introduced a 'no sitting' rule. Signs on headed notepaper now state: "Please refrain from sitting on the floor, due to health and safety. Thank you for your co-operation in the matter."

A tape barrier has also been placed along the edge of the step, which was popular with college students who could do homework there instead of having to spend money at cafes. The Ryemarket shopping centre, in Stourbridge, West Midlands, has just six benches to accommodate an estimated 70,000 customers each week. Ryemarket manager Kelley Dyas said the signs were put up because bags and outstretched legs were seen as a potential risk to passing shoppers. I tripped up once so I believe walking and standing poses a health problem as well. Oh, and lying prone in bed is also a health issue as I twisted my neck when I changed position. Oh dear oh dear and then there are various positions during the sexual act as well, need I go on?

TUESDAY 19TH MARCH 2013

Be warned, underwear can be very expensive especially used ones! A burglar with a sexual fetish for UNDERWEAR has been caught rifling through a homeowner's washing basket in search for his booty to satisfy his cravings. Unfortunately for him the homeowner disturbed him in the act and he made an escape scattering his desired objects as he fled. A man who admitted burgling a house in search of underwear has been jailed today. He pleaded guilty to breaking into a house to satisfy his unusual fetish and will go to prison for two years and ten months for stealing items from the washing-machine and washing basket. Apparently the homeowner did give chase but was forced to stop after he slipped over. Oh that reminds me, running is dangerous. Memo to supermarket to include that in its health and safety pamphlet! Anyway, the convicted "knicker nicker" will have plenty to sniff at when he joins the other inmates in prison. Perhaps he can get a job working in the laundry, sorting out the dirty boxers before they get washed.

THURSDAY 21TH MARCH 2013

Benefit cheats are the scourge of the nation and when caught they should be dealt with severely. It is just not the case they are cheats, they are stealing yours and mine hard earned money. Benefit fraud costs the nation £1.2 billion a year. Just think what that could do to build up this country again? A fraudster who pocketed £27,000 in benefits by claiming he couldn't walk escapes jail even after being caught on camera working as a delivery driver. The 47 year old told the Department of Work and Pensions (DWP) that he was 'in constant pain' and could not walk without a stick or support from someone else. The jury was shown covert video footage of him walking freely around Plymouth city centre in November 2009. After a three day trial he was convicted of failing to notify a change of circumstances that would affect his benefit claim. He was sentenced to 36 weeks in jail suspended for two years.

He said he is paying back the £27,626 and may take a considerable time if ever to pay it off - through deductions from his £80 a week benefits. To my mind any benefit cheat caught in the act should not ever receive any benefits from the country again. They have given up that right as soon as they embarked on illegal activities. A suspended sentence is not good enough for these scumbags. Asking them to pay the money back will never ever happen, although I firmly believe any items of value in their property such as HD Televisions, DVDs and vehicles should be sold at auction to help pay the money back to the state. Any money still in their bank accounts should also be confiscated and handed back to the state as well.

THURSDAY 21TH MARCH 2013

So, David Cameron is given a warning of the threat posed by the rise of the United Kingdom Independence Party (UKIP) as he enters a critical phase in the life of his government. Mr. Cameron perhaps you should actually ask the reason why there is a rise in people voting for UKIP. Is it because they are against wholesale immigration, is it because the benefit system is not fit for purpose and open to abuse from thousands of benefit cheats, is it because we are fighting wars in Afghanistan and Iraq which we should not be involved in, is it because you are getting us deeper and deeper in Syria whilst other Arab countries just look on, is it because individuals are better off on benefits than actually working, is it because the police force is underfunded and demoralised because of your disregard for law and order, is it because our once so proud fighting forces are being reduced to a token force, is it because ordinary working people are taxed way beyond their means, is it because you give away millions in foreign aid while people die needlessly in this country, is it because our school system has had its back broken by underfunding which has resulted in a generation of poorly educated and unruly children with a total disregard for authority, is it because we give billions to the EU when that money would be better spent in the UK. Need I say more, and you warn of the rise of UKIP? My answer to you is listen to the people before it is too late to save this once great country of ours.

FRIDAY 22TH MARCH 2013

The country is not going to the dogs it is going to benefit scroungers and cheats. Stephanie Demouh, originally from Togo, in West Africa, hold on a minute, which borough of London is that? lived in a four bedroom house, near Sloane Square, for about three years.However, after the government housing benefit was capped at £400-a-week she was moved into temporary accommodation 10-miles away by Westminster City Council. Mrs Demouh, who is studying accountancy at Westminster

University, believes she should be re-housed in the exclusive neighbourhood so her four children can attend a top Church of England school. I do not think so Stephanie. For a start I am not paying for you or your six offspring to enjoy your high life living on benefits. **PAY FOR IT YOURSELF!** And if you do not like it I can advise you of a flight back to Togo West Africa where I am sure you will be taken care off. In other words P**s O*f right now and pay your way in the world like the rest of us you scrounger!

SATURDAY 23RD MARCH 2013

Hot news, Britain's most tattooed man changes his name to Mr Body Art. Also known as the King of Inkland, he has 80% of his skin covered in designs – and has even had one of his eyeballs tattooed. Wow, impressed so far? He has also spent more than £20,000 and had at least 300 hours under the needle. Now Matt Whelan, 33 has changed his name by deed poll to Mr Body Art. The ex-wrestler, from Birmingham, says: "People who do what I do treat their body like a temple. Like Christians have Jesus, we have our bodies. "For my eyeball, I went to the opticians beforehand and got several opinions." He added: "When I die I want to leave my body to a museum. Someone in Canada has already asked to use my skull as a paint pot." I wonder if that could happen sooner than later or maybe it has happened already. As for changing his name perhaps Mr. Pratt with no brain would have been a better choice!

SUNDAY 24TH MARCH 2013

Yet another story about what is wrong with this country and this is just the tip of the religious iceberg. We are a Christian country and yet we are being penalised all the time. A Graphic artist has been turned down for work at an Essex hotel for being a Christian. He was told, "You can't work here, you'll upset the atheists" by a representative of the hotel after discovering he was a committed Christian. Quite rightly he is suing the hotel after claiming he was turned down for a job there because he is a Christian. He claims he was then told he would not be considered for the role as his beliefs could upset atheists working there. The row is the latest in a series of clashes between Christians and employers over their rights to express their faith in the workplace. But legal experts say this case is unprecedented because he apparently faced discrimination merely on the basis of his beliefs rather than his actions, such as wearing a cross. Apparently the hotel representatives have never heard of equal opportunities in Britain and that everyone should have an equal chance at getting a job. Oh silly me, equal opportunities is for atheists, Muslim's, foreigners, illegal immigrants, lesbians, gays and any other individuals and organisations that milk this country of our basic right to earn a living within our own shores. Again the government has lost its way and somewhere along the line lost its balls as well.

MONDAY 25TH MARCH 2013

In the news recently, Brits are too polite and scared of offending vocal and aggressive Muslims. A claim made by a former Obama adviser. The claims were made after a professor walked out of a debate hosted by an Islamic group at the University College London where organisers would not allow men and women to sit together. (As previously blogged) The professor said, "People are not only afraid to offend, but afraid to offend a vocal and aggressive group of people. Let me correct this thinking, we are not afraid to speak up against these thugs in the name of Islam, it is not us afraid to speak up against these racists who are trying to bully their way into this country. It is not us afraid to speak up against the murderers and bombers in the name of the Koran. It is this futile and weak government who are afraid to speak out in case they offend. So who cares if these outspoken people are offended? This is a democracy, the very democracy these aggressive Muslims are committed to get rid of and replace with Sharia law. The tide will turn and the Christian community will not be silent, with or without a gagged government.

TUESDAY 26TH MARCH 2013

Stupid Councillors! A Council has been accused of 'murdering' punctuation mark after abolishing apostrophes from street names. When council officers in a rural English district took the curious decision to do away with the apostrophe – because it caused "confusion" - they may have believed that the humble punctuation mark was too small and insignificant for anyone to care. But they have made a grave error. They have not taken into account the devotees of traditional grammar who came to its aid – and accused them of nothing short of "murder". The move was branded "appalling, disgusting and pointless", with one critic saying the absence of the marks made her "shudder". Some even suggested that it could represent a creeping threat that might even result in the endangerment of those grammatical stalwarts, the comma and the capital letter. Officials at Mid Devon council, ever alert to the perils of everyday life and eager to introduce new regulations, have proposed abolishing apostrophes from street names to "avoid potential confusion". A "risk assessment" had concluded that a policy on street names ought to be adopted, which formalised a long-standing practice in the district that they did not have apostrophes.

You stupid and ignorant councillors! We are talking about English grammar, which we supposedly teach our children in school. It is not up to you to change and modify it at a whim of a pathetic idea in the council chamber. Risk assessment? We need to have a risk assessment conducted on the dumb councillors as they are a danger to our valued English language. It is not up to you pathetic morons to modify the language which is set in stone. Samuel Johnson must be rolling in his grave and I hope he comes out of it and haunts you. The communications manager at the council said: "Our proposed policy on street naming and numbering covers a whole host of practical issues, many of which are aimed at reducing potential confusion over street names. "Although there is no national guidance that stops apostrophes being used, for many years the convention we've followed here is for new street names not to be given apostrophes." Communications Manager? I think not, you really do not know the difference between an apostrophe and your arse, and you get paid thousands for it. Do your job, do it right and do it correctly, without interfering with the English language.

WEDNESDAY 27TH MARCH 2013

Oh dear not too sure about this one! After the previous rants from Boris, Sir Peter Tapsell became the first Conservative MP to state that he would be prepared to give up his safe Commons seat to let Boris Johnson, the Mayor of London, return to Parliament. Sir Peter, 83, made the frank admission that he was "keeping his seat warm for Boris" to Mr Cameron personally in remarks overheard by several Tory MPs and, "the Mayor would be an excellent leader of the Opposition and perhaps a good prime minister. Recent weeks have seen a flurry of speculation about rival Tory candidates positioning themselves to succeed Mr Cameron — most recently Theresa May, the Home Secretary, who is believed by her colleagues to be "on manoeuvres". So there we have it then all in a nutshell, the Tories will be the opposition and Mr. Cameron is being replaced with a clown.

Ah, but which one, Boris or Theresa. Not a lot of choice I agree, but that is all the conservatives have got. What scares me is that Labour is even a worse bunch of clowns in an archaic big top which has already collapsed around them.

THURSDAY 28TH MARCH 2013

Stupid, stupid, stupid!

Home Secretary Theresa May has lost her appeal against a ruling preventing the deportation of preacher Abu Qatada. She acted after the Special Immigration Appeals Commission said the radical cleric could not be returned to Jordan. The judges said "he could face an unfair trial involving evidence obtained by torturing others." Well who the hell cares. This piece of dirt openly mocks this country and even glorifies the murder of British troops. He obtains millions of pounds in social benefit handouts and openly laughs about it. He is scum – **DEPORT HIM NOW.**

In this particular occurrence in this long sager surprisingly it was not government ministers who failed to act it was the stupid ill informed excuses of the judges. **SACK THEM NOW**. Lord Dyson, sitting with Lord Justice Richards and Lord Justice Elias, said the appeals commission was entitled to think there was a risk that the "impugned statements" would be admitted in evidence at a retrial. "In consequence, there is a real risk of a flagrant denial of justice," What a load of old twaddle, Abu Quatada is scum and must be deported from the very country he loathes so much.

FRIDAY 29TH MARCH 2013

As if Iraq and Afghanistan was not bad enough UK troops have started to arrive in Mali supposedly to train Malian soldiers as part of an EU training mission. The UK is also providing surveillance and logistical support to French troops who are helping the West African nation counter an Islamist insurgency. Mr. Hammond said: "Through this mission we will support the Malian government to counter the violent insurgency that has not only disrupted their country, but which also poses a clear threat to our national interests here in the UK." Does it? Now what national interests are they then? It is stupid and reckless of this government to deploy troops in yet another country which will never change in a million years. At the same time our once proud regiments of the armed forces are being cut to smithereens all in the name of cost cutting. Where do the savings go, to the influx of benefit seekers from Afghanistan, Iraq, Bulgaria, Romania and now most likely Mali. This government is out of date and ill informed. Either listen to the people of Britain, sack your advisers or let's have a change of government. The sands of time are quickly running through the hour glass!

SATURDAY 30TH MARCH 2013

Fifty years ago, the Beeching Report was published, spelling the end for thousands of stations and hundreds of branch lines. But now, in one corner of Britain, a new line is being laid that will restore a link cut by Beeching's axe. This is great news indeed. If it was not for Dr.Beeching this country would have one of the best railway infrastructures in the world.There would be fewer vehicles on the roads, reduced pollution and most likely a railway which would be affordable to travel on. What a concept that would be. In 1963 the railways criss-crossed Britain and even remote areas had stations. The Beeching report recommended taking an axe to about a third of the network - 5,000 miles of track, including hundreds of branch lines, 2,363 stations and tens of thousands of jobs. Improved bus services could replace branch lines, argued Dr Beeching. Wrong! There are doubts over his figures and in the end the railway never did make the savings he promised. Just another example of many, of the government being ill advised and not listening to the community they are supposed to be representing. Not a great deal has changed since 1963 then!!

Throughout my daily blog I have taken the opportunity to comment on a number of stories and news articles which have appeared in the national press. I have not made anything up and it is amazing what lunacy is going on around us. MP's appearing to act for themselves and not for the good of the people who they are supposed to represent. Councillors, who believe they are above the law, give themselves pay increases and raise the council tax to fund their own lifestyle.

Apparently Chancellor George Osborne did not realise a car he was travelling in was parked in a disabled bay at a motorway service station. Now forgive me but I thought there was big white sign painted on the road surface and usually another sign on a pole. Admittedly he was not driving the vehicle but he is a member of parliament and the vehicle was driven by a police officer. One law for us and one law for others!

Well not long now before Romanian and Bulgarian immigrants are allowed into our country after restrictions have been lifted. A new report has come up with conclusion that the migration to the UK will hit schools but have a lesser impact on housing. So let me get this right if the schools are going to be overcrowded that means that British school children will find it difficult to get a placement and thus a poorer education because of the immigrants.

As for the belief there will not be an impact on housing, of course there will be an impact on housing, do the children not have parents who need accommodation and thus further houses will need to be built for the use of immigrants. The policy needs to be changed NOW. Stop immigration NOW. We do not need any more waifs, strays, and gypsies stretching schools, housing and social services, never mind the social security benefits.

A father convicted of killing six of his children in a fire at his Derby house has been jailed for life, but I am sure he will be out before then. It just does not make sense that he will be out with good behaviour after 15 years and ready to claim welfare for all the other children he has sired as well. And why did he impreg so many woman? To claim the social benefits, that is why. He is scum and yet he was not doing anything illegal. The system was being used to claim thousands of pounds, how many more cases are there similar to this? Who is doing anything about it? **NOBODY!**

No wonder people in this country get upset when we rely on MPs and councillors to act for us, make policy and act accordingly. Unfortunately the system is being used and the good of the country is being forgotten. We need to act now before we are completely swallowed up and become the dump of Europe. I urge you to lobby your local councillors, MP and write to the current Prime Minister Mr. David Cameron voicing your concerns.

*****

A note from the author:

The motivation and drive for this publication came from the impact of what is happening to us all in this country. High taxation supposedly for austerity measures and yet we give millions of pounds away to other countries is so called aide. The working population funding lazy scroungers and benefit cheats. Immigration is at a level which is draining our resources and putting a strain on our schools and social services. Houses are being built on green belt land and floodplains, how stupid is that? Existing houses which can be renovated are left to rot and crumble. Commercial units built on farmland and left empty for years whilst others have still not been utilised. Madness! Due to the farming policy in this country, which is decided by Europe, farmers are going out of business and more and more of our food is imported from all over the world. What will happen the day certain countries do not export their crops any more, where do we go then? Grade "A" farming land is being taken over by fields of solar panels and wind turbines, the scourge of the countryside.

On a final note we had a structure of unique public houses in this country which was the envy of the world. They have been systematically destroyed by this and previous governments through extremely high taxation and greedy supermarkets selling cheap lager and beer as a loss leader. The community is being destroyed especially in towns and villages where this social activity is needed the most. Sit back, arms folded, feet up, whilst the rest of Europe wet their pants by their constant laughing at us!

The Chooooon collection Parts 1 and 2 available from Fast Print Publishing.

Both recordings are available from Amazon.

THE END – BUT ONLY JUST THE BEGINNING!

* 9 7 8 1 7 8 0 3 5 6 1 6 7 *
ND - #0097 - 110926 - C109 - 297/210/5 - PB - 9781780356167 - Gloss Lamination